Aligning Security Operations with the MITRE ATT&CK Framework

Level up your security operations center for better security

Rebecca Blair

BIRMINGHAM—MUMBAI

Aligning Security Operations with the MITRE ATT&CK Framework

Group Product Manager: Pavan Ramchandani

Publishing Product Manager: Prachi Sawant

Senior Editor: Runcil Rebello

Technical Editor: Arjun Varma

Copy Editor: Safis Editing

Project Coordinator: Ashwin Kharwa

Proofreader: Safis Editing

Indexer: Tejal Daruwale Soni

Production Designer: Prashant Ghare

Marketing Coordinator: Agnes D'souza

First published: May 2023

Production reference: 01280423

Published by Packt Publishing Ltd.

Livery Place

35 Livery Street

Birmingham

B3 2PB, UK.

ISBN 978-1-80461-426-6

www.packtpub.com

To my colleagues both past and present, thank you for your mentorship and cooperation. To my friends, thank you for the support and for pushing me to be who I am, especially Tyler and hype-woman Jennifer. To my family, Emily, Alex, and Gadget, thank you for your patience and support; without it, this book would not have been completed. To countless others not mentioned, thank you.

– Rebecca Blair

Contributors

About the author

Rebecca Blair has, for over a decade, focused on working in and building up **security operations center (SOC)** teams. She has had the unique experience of building multiple teams from scratch and scaling them for growth and 24/7 operations. She currently serves as the manager of the SOC, corporate security, and **network operations center (NOC)** at a Boston-based tech company, and as a cyber educational content creator for N2K Networks. She previously worked as the director of SOC operations at IronNet, a lead technical validator, a watch officer, and an SOC analyst for various government contractors. She has a bachelor of science degree in computer security and information assurance from Norwich University, a master of science degree in cybersecurity from the University of Maryland Global Campus, and a master of business degree in administration from Villanova University.

About the reviewer

Allen Ramsay has worked in the cyber trenches in 24/7 SOCs for most of his career. He has specialized in network defense and alert triage. He has previously contributed to multiple articles for *SC* magazine and has been a contributing author to *The Rook's Guide to C++*. He has a bachelor of science in computer security and information assurance from Norwich University and a master of science degree in cyber forensics and counterterrorism from the University of Maryland Global Campus.

Table of Contents

Part 2 – Detection Improvements and Alignment with ATT&CK

5

A Deep Dive into the ATT&CK Framework   45

6

Strategies to Map to ATT&CK   77

Preface

Hi, infosec professionals! This book is for cyber security professionals that are interested in SOC operations and/or are currently working in SOC operations. It is also for those interested in learning about the MITRE ATT&CK framework and bridges the gap between theoretical and practical knowledge through the use of examples, implementations, and detections.

There are three main portions to this book. They are as follows:

- The Basics – SOC and ATT&CK – Two Worlds in a Delicate Balance

- Detection Improvements and Alignment with ATT&CK

- Continuous Improvement and Innovation

There are various resources out there about different tools that map to MITRE, as well as the MITRE ATT&CK framework, which is fully publicly available online at `https://attack.mitre.org/`. What sets this book apart is that it takes practical knowledge of how to set up your environment and an in-depth review of the MITRE ATT&CK framework and explains how you can apply that framework to your environment.

Who this book is for

This book is for security professionals of all levels. It is focused on SOC environments but also covers some compliance, purple team exercises, threat hunting, and so on. It can be used to help build new security programs, as well as level up and assess the maturity of your current program.

What this book covers

Chapter 1, *SOC Basics – Structure, Personnel, Coverage, and Tools*, introduces the landscape of the SOC, which is a critical team in security and can have many different roles and sub-teams. We'll discuss SOC basics such as alert triaging, creating detections, incident response, and "trust but verify," as well as how it can interact with other teams or have sub-teams. This information is important because depending on the environment, you'll be able to apply different aspects of ATT&CK.

Chapter 2, *Analyzing your Environment for Potential Pitfalls*, discusses techniques for critically reviewing your processes, coverage, and systems, and provides advice on potential problem areas. By following this, the reader will be able to directly apply it to their environments to look for areas of improvement and avoid any pitfalls; it will also be helpful when looking to implement ATT&CK.

Chapter 3, Reviewing Different Threat Models, reviews multiple different threat models, their use cases, and their advantages and disadvantages. Doing so will allow the reader to apply the one that makes the most sense for their environment; the chapter also provides a comparison point to compare those threat models to ATT&CK.

Chapter 4, What is the ATT&CK Framework?, outlines the evolution of the ATT&CK framework and the various different high-level configurations for types of systems (i.e. cloud, mobile, Windows, etc.). It will also be the first introduction to related use cases.

Chapter 5, A Deep Dive into the ATT&CK Framework, provides a deeper look at the different techniques that are covered by the framework, and potential gaps within the framework. The reader will understand how to rank different techniques and their applicability to their own environments. This will focus specifically on the cloud, Windows, Mac, and network frameworks.

Chapter 6, Strategies to Map to ATT&CK, discusses how to analyze your environment, identify coverage gaps, and identify areas for improvement. Then, we'll cover how to map those gaps to the ATT&CK framework, to increase coverage and build out maturity in your security posture.

Chapter 7, Common Mistakes with Implementation, presents an overview of common mistakes that I have personally made in mappings and detections, as well as areas where I've seen others make mistakes. That way, you can learn from our shortcomings and implement mappings the right way.

Chapter 8, Return on Investment Detections, explains how creating detections and alerts is the bread and butter of any SOC environment. It should not be a surprise to anyone that less-than-stellar detections are created/triggered on a daily basis. This chapter will discuss alerts that we have had the highest efficiency ratings on, as well as the lowest, and how to measure their success.

Chapter 9, What Happens After an Alert is Triggered?, covers how once an alert is triggered, in theory, a set of actions begins. This chapter will discuss the different sets of actions, how to create playbooks, and how to ultimately triage alerts.

Chapter 10, Validating Any Mappings and Detections, argues that the most important step you can take to help yourself is setting up a review process. This can be completed manually, or you can create an automated feedback loop to track the efficiency ratings of your mappings and make improvements when necessary.

Chapter 11, Implementing ATT&CK in All Parts of Your SOC, goes through how to narrow down your environment and prioritize where you need to fix a coverage area. The chapter will then outline how you can implement detections and the ATT&CK framework as part of your overall security posture, and how it can be applied to teams outside of the SOC as well.

Chapter 12, What's Next? Areas for Innovation in Your SOC, points out some key areas that can take a SOC from basic to mature, covering topics such as scalability and automation. This chapter will include ideas that I had for innovating my own SOC but also interviews with other industry professionals and what they think needs to be done to achieve innovation.

To get the most out of this book

This book can apply to all types of SOC environments, and while no specific software is required, there are multiple examples that use Log Correlation or Security Information Event Management (SIEM) tools, as well as Search Orchestration Automation and Response (SOAR) tools. This book will also cover matrices for multiple operating systems such as Windows, Linux, macOS, network, mobile, and so on, so a base understanding of those types of operating systems and environments would be helpful but not necessary.

Software/hardware covered in the book	Operating system requirements
MITRE ATT&CK framework	Windows, macOS, or Linux
SOAR tools (Insight Connect)	
SIEM (Splunk)	
Amazon Web Services (AWS)	

Download the color images

We also provide a PDF file that has color images of the screenshots and diagrams used in this book. You can download it here: `https://packt.link/Cy0Jj`

Conventions used

There are a number of text conventions used throughout this book.

`Code in text`: Indicates code words in text, database table names, folder names, filenames, file extensions, pathnames, dummy URLs, user input, and Twitter handles. Here is an example: "Screen Capture is carried out by an attacker utilizing the `screencap`, `screenrecord`, or `MediaProjectionManager` commands."

A block of code is set as follows:

```
index=network_data size= (bytes_out/1024) size>= 100 | table _time,
user, size
```

Bold: Indicates a new term, an important word, or words that you see onscreen. For instance, words in menus or dialog boxes appear in **bold**. Here is an example: "A tactic in the ATT&CK framework for the enumeration of shares can be found at **Network Share Discovery**."

> **Tips or important notes**
> Appear like this.

Get in touch

Feedback from our readers is always welcome.

General feedback: If you have questions about any aspect of this book, email us at `customercare@packtpub.com` and mention the book title in the subject of your message.

Errata: Although we have taken every care to ensure the accuracy of our content, mistakes do happen. If you have found a mistake in this book, we would be grateful if you would report this to us. Please visit `www.packtpub.com/support/errata` and fill in the form.

Piracy: If you come across any illegal copies of our works in any form on the internet, we would be grateful if you would provide us with the location address or website name. Please contact us at `copyright@packt.com` with a link to the material.

If you are interested in becoming an author: If there is a topic that you have expertise in and you are interested in either writing or contributing to a book, please visit `authors.packtpub.com`.

Share Your Thoughts

Once you've read *Aligning Security Operations with the MITRE ATT&CK Framework*, we'd love to hear your thoughts! Scan the QR code below to go straight to the Amazon review page for this book and share your feedback.

https://packt.link/r/1804614262

Your review is important to us and the tech community and will help us make sure we're delivering excellent quality content.

Download a free PDF copy of this book

Thanks for purchasing this book!

Do you like to read on the go but are unable to carry your print books everywhere? Is your eBook purchase not compatible with the device of your choice?

Don't worry, now with every Packt book you get a DRM-free PDF version of that book at no cost.

Read anywhere, any place, on any device. Search, copy, and paste code from your favorite technical books directly into your application.

The perks don't stop there, you can get exclusive access to discounts, newsletters, and great free content in your inbox daily

Follow these simple steps to get the benefits:

1. Scan the QR code or visit the link below

https://packt.link/free-ebook/978-1-80461-426-6

2. Submit your proof of purchase
3. That's it! We'll send your free PDF and other benefits to your email directly

Part 1 – The Basics: SOC and ATT&CK, Two Worlds in a Delicate Balance

The first part of this book will provide you with the basics. This means that it will cover what goes into a **SOC**, or **Security Operations Center**, including the teams and key roles that play a key part in security operations, and some of the teams that a SOC works closely with. Then, you will learn how to analyze your environments for security gaps and gain an understanding of a few different threat models that could be applied to your environment. As a send-off for the first part, we will cover an introduction to the ATT&CK framework, and we will cover it in more depth in the following parts.

This part has the following chapters:

- *Chapter 1, SOC Basics – Structure, Personnel, Coverage, and Tools*
- *Chapter 2, Analyzing Your Environment for Potential Pitfalls*
- *Chapter 3, Reviewing Different Threat Models*
- *Chapter 4, What Is the ATT&CK Framework?*

SOC Basics – Structure, Personnel, Coverage, and Tools

In this chapter, we will cover the landscape of what your average **security operation center** (**SOC**) looks like. We'll discuss the structure of the specific roles within the SOC and possible sub-teams that can feed into or be part of the SOC environment. We'll discuss strategies for alert triage, creating detections, incident response, and other important functions such as "trust but verify," and how these functions can promote cross-team collaboration and apply to all aspects of the business. Having a strong understanding of the SOC can be critical to applying the various aspects of the ATT&CK framework. This will also allow you to evaluate the SOC environments that you might work in or interact with, and suggest possible changes, improvements, or areas for expansion. This chapter is comprised of the following sections:

- SOC environments and roles
- SOC environment responsibilities
- SOC coverage
- SOC cross-team collaboration

Technical requirements

For this chapter, there are no installations or specific technologies that are required.

SOC environments and roles

The SOC environment is one of the most critical teams that comprises your organization's security posture. At the same time, there is no true one-size-fits-all for any SOC environment, which is part of the fun when evaluating yours for improvements. So how do you evaluate how your SOC should be set up? Well, that depends on the purpose of your organization. To test that theory, we will discuss a few hypothetical companies and the make-up of a few different SOC teams that I have seen first-hand. We'll also talk through important traits for any SOC employee and drill down to specific roles.

SOC environments, as mentioned, all look different, but at the core, they are responsible for alert triage and incident response. In some cases, they can also be responsible for red team activities, security engineering, and network monitoring. That means that your basic roles are *SOC analysts*, *incident responders*, and *SOC managers*, but again that changes depending on scope. Expanded SOC environments might have **network operations center** (**NOC**) *managers*, *NOC analysts*, *security engineers*, *threat intelligence analysts*, or *red team operators*.

The first hypothetical SOC that we will evaluate is for a company called Blair Consulting. Blair Consulting has a SOC that is responsible for the management of security tools for building detections and for tabletop exercises, and they also have a hybrid environment, which means that there is a combination of on-premises systems and cloud systems. A SOC at that company would be comprised of a SOC manager, incident responder, security engineers, a red team specialist or engineer, and a cloud security engineer. The specific number of people would depend on the size of the organization, but as a rule of thumb, I try to have 1 incident responder for every 200–300 employees. That number primarily takes effect after you have a base set of employees for your team, which is done in the scaling-up period. This also changes if you are a public or private company because if you are public, or depending on the types of data your organization has, you might have reporting requirements for incidents, such as reporting to credit card bureaus in the case of a breach that concerns payment card industry data.

As you can see, any environment will require different teams and personnel, and no one environment looks the same. You should base it on the resources your organization has, the risks that have been identified as high and critical for your organization, and the projected growth/scalability of both the team and the organization.

SOC environment responsibilities

A SOC environment can have varying responsibilities. At the core, you have an incident response and alert triage. To accomplish comprehensive incident response, you want to have a strategy for 24/7 coverage, which can be accomplished by having a larger team and having shift patterns, partnering with a **managed service security provider** (**MSSP**), implementing a follow-the-sun model, or using an on-call roster. The option that you choose depends on the resources and infrastructure your team has. For example, if the organization has multiple offices located around the world, you would want to implement a follow-the-sun model, where you have multiple SOC analysts located at each office so that they can work their respective 9–5 type shift, and due to the various time zones and the addition of a few weekend shifts, that will give you the 24x7 coverage envisaged by the follow-the-sun model. The advantages of using an MSSP would give you the advantage of having a smaller in-house team while having support for alert triage and 24x7 coverage, but of course, that comes with a typically high price tag.

If you do everything out of one office and in multiple shifts, you would typically see 4 different shifts of 12 hours, A Day, A Night, B Day, B Night, where in 1 week, members assigned to A Day and A Night work for 4 days with 12-hour shifts, and the ones assigned to B Day and B Night work 3 days with 12-hour shifts, Each week, it would flip for the team that worked weekends.

The following chart will help you envision this:

Day Number	7am-7pm (Day Shift)	7pm-7am(Night Shift)
1-Monday	Shift A Day	Shift A Night
2-Tuesday	Shift A Day	Shift A Night
3-Wednesday	Shift B Day	Shift B Night
4-Thursday	Shift B Day	Shift B Night
5-Friday	Shift B Day	Shift B Night
6-Saturday	Shift A Day	Shift A Night
7-Sunday	Shift A Day	Shift A Night
8-Monday	Shift B Day	Shift B Night
9-Tuesday	Shift B Day	Shift B Night
10-Wednesday	Shift B Day	Shift B Night
11-Thursday	Shift A Day	Shift A Night
12-Friday	Shift A Day	Shift A Night
13-Saturday	Shift A Day	Shift A Night
14-Sunday	Shift B Day	Shift B Night

Figure 1.1 – 2-week 4-shift rotation schedule

The benefit of that is that in a 14-day time period, you only work 7 days, but again they are 12-hour shifts. You'll see this type of setup in a lot of government SOC environments. The final option is to just use an on-call roster. In theory, if a high-severity alert is triggered or someone needs to trigger the incident response process, they would use a call roster or a tool such as Ops Genie, which would page whoever is on call. While this is the cheapest option for coverage, it does come with a higher level of risk that alerts will go untriaged, or incidents might take longer to contain or mitigate. In my experience, I'll typically start a new SOC environment following the on-call method while processes are established, and then as the organization and SOC mature, I'll either contract with an MSSP or hire enough staff to use the follow-the-sun method.

In addition to incident response, another core responsibility is alert triage. To have alerts, you need to also establish detections that can be completed by SOC analysts or dedicated detection engineers. Alert triaging can sound boring and monotonous, but it is a situation where you are constantly solving a different puzzle. It's the responsibility of the SOC to create alerts to be able to effectively analyze the logs to find potentially suspicious actions or traffic. The purpose of that is that it is not effective or scalable to be analyzing raw logs all day; the rate at which suspicious actions would be missed is astronomical. Therefore, in theory, it is a key responsibility to have the ability to create complex alerts, which ideally pull in information from various data sources to essentially complete the first few steps of triage for your analysts. You also need to test alerts and review them regularly for efficiency because you do not want your analysts to spend all day triaging false positive alerts. Another aspect that can help with this responsibility is setting up some type of case management system to ensure that analysts do not duplicate efforts by triaging the same alert, and that would allow you to track metrics such as time to ticket, time to triage, and time to mitigation, which can help you drive initiatives for your team.

Threat intelligence analysts can be like security engineers or other types of roles in the SOC, the same way that a SOC analyst might perform some threat intelligence activities such as conducting operational intelligence research, which would provide contextual information for potentially suspicious IPs, domains, URLs, among other types of activities. A threat intelligence analyst conducts research on a larger scale. Some of their responsibilities might include integrating threat feeds such as ones from Abuse.ch, FireEye, and GoPhish (there are literally hundreds of both public and private threat feeds) or creating a deny list of hashes or domains based on triage findings, which can be applied to your organization's firewall or endpoint detection and response tools. Another responsibility of a threat intelligence analyst is to stay current on all cyber threats, advanced persistent threat groups, and vulnerabilities, which may include writing threat reports on vulnerabilities that apply to the organization or industry.

The NOC is a part of the SOC or can be its own team. The NOC contains team members called NOC analysts, who have similar responsibilities to SOC analysts. They are responsible for monitoring networks; however, they can be less security-focused. A great example of a NOC is where it monitors smaller managed networks and remediates or investigates changes that might not align with a golden image, or reviews whether a change management process was followed properly for any network changes. If a network change might be suspicious, the NOC would work closely with the SOC to triage and assist where needed in the incident response process.

Security engineers can have a multitude of responsibilities. First, they can assist with creating detections and alerts for analysts. Next, they work heavily on the concept of "trust but verify." This means that you trust employees with the best of intentions, but review configurations to ensure that they are secure. One common example is that when testing in a development environment, it's very easy to stand up a new Amazon **Elastic Cloud Computer** (**EC2**) instance or create a new security group and in the interest of time, leave its firewall rules wide open to the internet. A security engineer would ideally have alerts set up to trigger when a new overly permissive group is stood up and work with that initial person to restrict the group as needed for the project.

Red team operators similarly can be their own team and work closely with security engineers and the SOC or fully be part of the SOC. Red team engineers or operators typically work on offensive operations tasks such as penetration testing, purple team testing, and assisting with trust-but-verify. The penetration testing responsibility and purple teaming go hand in hand. A **purple team exercise** is where a penetration test is being conducted via a set of pre-specified use cases, and the SOC analysts are notified when the testing is going to begin, its status, and so on. That way, it is a collaborative effort to test out any detections and coverage and provide an opportunity to improve.

Managers of sub-teams or of the SOC, or really any leadership role as part of the overall SOC, needs to be unique. They of course must handle administrative tasks, such as capturing metrics, creating reports, and personnel management, but they also must have a strong technical background to be effective. They must plan out a roadmap that addresses the risk of the organization, allows the team to grow and follow a scalable model, while also supporting the team members. To provide for proper growth and planning, the managers should be able to project the next 6 months of roadmaps. I recommend planning out no more than 60% of your time for projects depending on the role, to account for interrupts such as incidents or unforeseen complications and be flexible in the amount of work or types of projects projected to allow for necessary pivots.

SOC environments clearly have many varying roles and responsibilities, which really depend on the specifics of your organization and environment. You should identify the expected responsibilities of your SOC and ensure that you have enough personnel with the correct skill set or potentially provide training to develop the needed skill sets to fill any role. For scaling purposes, I typically try to add one SOC analyst and one security engineer per 500 employees, 1 NOC analyst per 5,000 network assets, 1–3 total red team engineers, 1 threat intelligence analyst for every 1,000 employees, 1 manager for every 5–10 SOC employees, and a senior manager or director as needed. Of course, this is just a general rule of thumb and can be tweaked to meet your needs.

SOC coverage

Expanding coverage and using your data effectively is critically important to any SOC's ability to carry out its responsibilities. With a lack of coverage or visibility, the SOC will have nothing to monitor or detect, and your organization will have a significantly higher risk level because of it. That's why it is an important factor within a SOC to determine the current level of coverage, where the gaps are, how to prioritize the gaps, and how to fill those gaps by increasing coverage.

The first stage is to determine what level of coverage you currently have. Regardless of whether your organization is a newer SOC or a more established one, I make it a point to baseline coverage before making any other roadmap decisions. To do so, I take note of all data sources that are being ingested into whatever **security information event management (SIEM)** is in use, such as Splunk or ELK, and I write down and organize all alerts by function. In addition to this, I review or create a risk registry that categorizes the highest risks that face the organization and, if time permits, conduct a purple team exercise. As explained in the *SOC environment responsibilities* section for a red team engineer role, and will be further explained in future chapters, a purple team exercise is a joint project where offensive operations are carried out to test the visibility and efficiency of alerts in place. This can also be useful in proving the negative, which means proving that attacks can be conducted without any visibility, which helps push the importance of increasing coverage.

After you have determined where the gaps are, you need to prioritize them and create a plan on how to fix them. One of the strategies for prioritizing is to list out the types of logs and visibility each missing source would give. For example, if you are not capturing logs from your organization's **Virtual Private Network (VPN)**, and it's a remote work environment, then you have limited visibility into User browsing logs. You would then write out the risks or potential attacks that could be discovered with those logs and write down any mitigations. For example, while you might not capture user browsing logs but capture endpoint detection and response logs, you'll still have some visibility into the applications used, and downloads, so that might lower the risk of not capturing those initial logs. Another strategy is after writing down the missing sources and suspected size of the logs, to prioritize them based on an effort to ingest them. For example, if you can download an app on your SIEM, utilize an API key and creds, and everything is managed in-house, then as long as the size of the logs isn't the problem, you should be able to easily configure the new ingest. I typically recommend picking a mix of harder-to-implement logs to start the process for ingest while also implementing a few that are considered a quick win. Another way to prioritize coverage gaps is based on what you are prepared to write detections for or base it on team expertise. That way, you know whatever source of data that gets added will immediately be used to increase coverage because, in theory, you don't want to waste licensing space, time, or money if you can't take advantage of the additional coverage.

Filling any coverage gaps after prioritization can be done by expanding your ingest license for your current SIEM tool or using a data lake to capture additional logs without ingest in your SIEM tool. Therefore, you'll still be able to run analytics and only ingest absolutely necessary data within your SIEM tool. Expanding your resources and current license seems like the simplest path, but a common issue with that path is that it can be cost-prohibitive. That's where other solutions such as log tiering or using a data lake come into play. By implementing a different technical solution, such as a data lake through providers such as Snowflake, you are able to have logs transferred and collected in a centralized location, and then run analytics over those logs, and only ingest detections on a subset of the logs. That way, you have the coverage, but your ingest costs are lower. One of the downsides to this approach is that you need to implement a new technical implementation, connectors, and so on, and that, of course, has its own costs associated with it. Of course, any approach that is taken to fill a coverage gap is reliant on proper cross-team collaboration.

Coverage is always an ongoing battle as your company grows and gains capabilities. It's important to regularly evaluate your coverage for improvements and to document any gaps, as this will help your SOC team mature. As mentioned, there are multiple ways to evaluate coverage and identify gaps, which will allow you to make an action plan for how to remediate those gaps.

SOC cross-team collaboration

"Alone we can do so little; together we can do so much" – Helen Keller.

This quote applies to the SOC environment as much as it does to most of life. One of the key functions that the SOC needs to be involved in will be promoting cross-team collaboration. This can be applied to all individual teams and functions of SOCs. For example, an analyst might triage an alert about suspicious DNS calls. While they can speculate on whether it's DNS poisoning or a possible misconfiguration, they really need to reach out and work with a networking team to be able to fully triage and get to the root cause of what caused that alert. Similarly, in a trust-but-verify role, a cloud security engineer in the SOC would need to work with the infrastructure team, or potential development operations teams, which will be the ones standing up the initial cloud resources.

One of the key responsibilities of the SOC is "trust but verify," and that relies on the principle of least privilege. The reasoning is that you want someone independent of the change to have the ability to validate the security behind it, so there is a lack of conflict of interest. In general, you would want security implemented by design, and the SOC or subsequent teams should coordinate to discuss security implementations prior to implementing any changes, which would shorten the validation period.

Other responsibilities, such as purple teaming exercises, are an inherently collaborative effort because they require multiple personnel of different roles to work together. As mentioned in the previous section, they primarily require a red team engineer to work collaboratively with other teams. We'll also cover purple team exercises in depth in future chapters. Similarly, incident response efforts regularly require cross-team collaboration work in the mitigation stages. The reason is that in the case of a **distributed denial-of-service** (**DDoS**) attack, the SOC team might not be the one to implement firewall rule changes; they might have to work with a network engineer to implement changes. Or if the SOC works in an engineering environment, they might have to work with the respective engineering teams to implement CAPTCHAs, restrict logins, and so on.

There are many cases where the SOC is only able to conduct their work through effective cross-team collaboration. That effort provides a more security-informed workforce, and while issues might arise due to differing opinions on technical implementations, restraints, or even personalities, it's critical that the lines of communication remain open and that all teams continue to work together.

Cross-team collaboration is critical for any team, but especially for a SOC. The reason is that the SOC must work with time-sensitive and potentially damaging incidents and data. The SOC is also responsible for maturing the security posture of the organization and ensuring that the principle of least privilege is in place; that can only be accomplished through cross-team collaboration. There are many times when a suspected incident turns out to be a misconfiguration, and by reaching out to other teams such as a network engineering team, your SOC will be more efficient and have the ability to triage more alerts.

Summary

To summarize, no two SOCs will ever be the same, and this can be inherently complex at first. Once you break it down and identify the needs of the organization, you will be able to determine what roles are needed and what the minimum size for your SOC is so that you can scale appropriately. Once you have at least some of the roles in place, you must evaluate your coverage so that you can identify your coverage gaps, and what the risks are for your organization. From there, you can remediate those gaps and risks through increased logging, increased detection engineering, or making technical changes. The increase in coverage is typically only accomplished through cross-team collaboration, which also makes the SOC team more efficient and ensures that proper access controls such as the principle of least privilege remain in place.

In the next chapter, we'll take a deeper look at identifying risks through creating a risk registry, making a test plan, and conducting a purple team exercise, and hear from an industry analyst about common gaps and shortfalls. All of this will involve practical information, which you will be able to implement in your SOC environment to help increase your organization's security maturity.

2

Analyzing Your Environment for Potential Pitfalls

This chapter will discuss techniques for critically reviewing your processes, coverage, and systems, and provide advice on potential problem areas. By doing this, you will be able to directly apply it to your environments to look for areas of improvement and avoid any pitfalls, and it will be helpful when looking to implement the ATT&CK framework.

In this chapter, we will cover the following topics:

- Danger! Risks ahead – how to establish a risk registry
- Red and blue make purple – how to run purple team exercises
- Discussing common coverage gaps and security shortfalls

Technical requirements

No installations or specific technologies are required for this chapter.

Danger! Risks ahead – how to establish a risk registry

Risks are a common part of life, and security is no different. If anything, in my opinion, security teams operate with more risk than other business units. Therefore, as part of a security program and SOC, you'll need to be able to effectively evaluate and measure risks, and build and manage a risk registry.

To start, you need to identify risks and determine whether they should be tracked on a risk registry. While personnel who are already experienced in information security probably already understand what a risk register is, there are many ways to complete it. This is an example of what I would recommend for setting up and evaluating a registry. The first step in identifying risks is to review whether there are currently any threat models or risks identified. If you are in an already established program, those responsible for it should have an idea of what the potential risks are, and what the common threat vectors are that they face. If the organization is new or still needs to mature its security program, you should talk a look at your asset lists and any technical areas connecting to the internet. For example, for email, especially in cases where **Domain-based Message Authentication, Reporting, and Conformance (DMARC)**, **Sender Policy Frameworks (SPFs)**, or **DomainKeys Identified Mail (DKIM)** are configured and enabled, you are at a higher risk of phishing emails, which is a common threat in any environment, but would be ranked as a higher threat if mitigations such DMARC, SPFs, and DKIM were not in place. For those that might not know, DMARC is an email authentication protocol that can be enabled and allows for greater protection from email spoofing. Similarly, SPFs are also email authentication protocols, which, when enabled, help detect forged email senders. DKIM is an authentication method that helps identify when forged senders are used, which is indicative of email spoofing.

Another example is if you are in a strictly cloud development environment, you will want to ensure that your storage buckets are encrypted, and you have proper **Access Control Lists (ACLs)** in place. ACLs are sets of rules that state what users, systems, traffic, ports, and so on are allowed access to a specific system or network, such as a cloud instance. If you do not have encryption or correct ACLs in place, then you are at a higher risk of unauthorized access and unintentional information disclosure, and this would be a higher risk on your registry as well.

After looking at the asset list and identifying the potential low-hanging fruit, you need to enter the trust-but-verify stage. While this was covered in *Chapter 1*, *SOC Basics – Structure, Personnel, Coverage, and Tools*, this is critically important. It's important to go into any situation and assume good intent, which means that you suspect no one is intentionally causing a security gap; however, it's very common for security gaps to be implemented in the interest of trying to deploy code quickly because of general oversight or because of tight deadlines and limited resources. As a security practitioner, you should evaluate your current environment and determine where there are areas for risks. For example, if you are a cloud security engineer and you want to evaluate a cloud environment, you might use the open source tool **Prowler** (`https://github.com/prowler-cloud/prowler`), which can be used to scan an AWS environment in accordance with different compliance frameworks for security best practices and help you establish your security baseline and subsequent areas for threats.

Throughout the process of identifying risks, you need to document them and give them subsequent ratings and severity scores. As you can see, the following screenshot is an example of a risk registry document:

Blair Organization Risk Registry	
Risk ID	SI-7
Business Area	Engineering
Title	Log4j
Description	From a recent vulnerability scan, 15 systems vulnerable to the Log4j vulnerability were discovered.
Category	Vulnerability
Root Cause (if known)	An old version of Java is operational on the systems. The Log4j vulnerability was discovered as a zero-day vulnerability. The systems were never originally patched due to being legacy technology, which would become non-operational if updated.
Impact	3
Likelihood	4
Risk Score	12
Treatment Strategy	Mitigated
Compensating Controls (if any)	The systems are internal only and do not have any connections to the internet.
Risk Owner	CTO
Status	Deferred
Notes	Tracked in JIRA-001

Table 2.1 – Risk registry example

The categories we have listed on our risk registry are as follows:

- **Risk ID**: This could be a numerical system to track risks at your organization; I've used this to show a related compliance control – for example, CM-6b from the Risk Management Framework (*NIST 800-53 standard*).

- **Business Area**: This depends on the size of your organization; if you have a larger organization this would identify the specific business unit, such as customer-facing, or a product line. If you work in a smaller organization, you might change this to a specific team, or get rid of the column.

- **Title**: (Self-explanatory.) This is the title of the risk. If it is for a specific vulnerability, you might put *Log4j for X systems*, and use the specific vulnerability name. In general, you want to use a specific name to help identify the risk.

- **Description**: In this area, you want to lay out the risk. That means you type out how many systems it could potentially impact, how this risk being compromised might affect your organization, and whether this risk is due to a vulnerability, supply chain issue, known factor, and so on.

- **Category**: Here is where you would list whether the risk is compliance-related, operational, strategic, and so on. On the other hand, I have seen risks categorized as what their root threat vector might be: for example, the user base or email.

- **Root Cause (if known)**: You want to document whether this is a vulnerability or risk related to a third party, whether its root cause is due to an incident, or whether it's due to a lack of coverage. Fill in as much information as possible because that will help with identifying what mitigating steps will need to be taken.

- **Impact**: This is a number rating, typically between 1 and 5 (1 - Very Low, 2 - Low, 3 - Moderate, 4 - High, 5 - Very High). The number is chosen based on what would happen if the risk was discovered or compromised.

- **Likelihood**: This is also a number rating, typically between 1 and 5 (1 - Very Low, 2 - Low, 3 - Moderate, 4 - High, 5 - Very High). The number is chosen based on what would happen if the risk was discovered or compromised.

- **Risk Score**: For the risk score, you multiply the rating from **Likelihood** and **Impact** together to get a risk score between 1 and 25. The higher the number, the greater the risk.

- **Treatment Strategy**: This is your planned action. It could be as simple as just putting **Mitigated**, **Accepted**, **Deferred**, or **Denied**, or including all information on steps needed to take to mitigate or close out the risk.

- **Compensating Controls (if any)**: This is where you list out any steps that have already been taken to mitigate or control the risk. You can also list out future actions; just make sure that they are marked as **Pending** until they are completed.

- **Risk Owner**: This would be the person responsible for accepting any risk. Essentially, every risk should be assigned to someone (it could be your CIO, CISO, and so on) to accept that it is a risk, and ideally help work toward mitigation.

- **Status**: This is the current status and could be listed as **In Progress**, **Deferred**, **Unchanged**, and so on.

- **Notes**: In this section, I note whether there are any case management tickets associated with the risks and whether there have been any changes in owners, work completed, status, and so on.

Regarding the numerical rating system for the **impact**, **Likelihood**, and eventual **risk score** categories, the higher the number, the greater the risk. Another way to determine or show the risk score is shown in *Figure 2.1* by taking the same **Impact** and **Likelihood** values:

Likelihood	1- Impacts Single User or System	Impact			
		2- Impacts < 10 users or no more than 25% of all users	3 - Impacts > 10 users but < 50 or no more than 50% of all users	4- Impacts > 50% of users but there is no PII data	5-Impacts > 50% of Users and PII Data or Impacts >70% with no PII
1- 1%-5%	Very Low	Very Low	Very Low	Low	Low
2- 5%-15%	Very Low	Low	Low	Moderate	Moderate
3 - 15%-35%	Low	Low	Moderate	High	High
4- 35%-85%	Low	Moderate	High	Very High	Very High
5- 85%-100%	Moderate	High	High	Very High	Very High

Figure 2.1 – Risk score identification

As you can see from the chart, we added some basic standards for how to determine what numbers to use for the ratings and a generalization around what level the risk would be at. One thing to keep in mind is the type of data that would be impacted. For example, if any **Personally Identifiable Information (PII)** is included in the breach, you must automatically increase the impact number, because due to privacy regulations and general security standards, you must protect PII. Do so similarly with **Payment Card Industry (PCI)** data or with **Health Insurance Portability and Accountability Act (HIPAA)** health data. Make sure to understand the data that you are housing and transmitting in your organization to be able to effectively categorize your risk.

The other part that goes into calculation is the proper evaluation of risk. This can be done via researching the risk, which can be done by walking through Tabletop Exercises (TTX), It can be measured by performing purple team exercises; it could even be measured by exploiting the risk in a lab. For example, if your risk was phishing, you could run phishing tests throughout your organization to test your workforce and measure the percentage of users that click on harmful links

After the risk registry is created, an owner for the document and process needs to be established. That owner could be someone in the SOC, it could be the CISO themselves, or it could be someone from the legal or compliance departments. That way, there is one person or team that oversees updating and maintaining the registry. The registry should also be reviewed with all applicable stakeholders on a quarterly basis to ensure that it is up to date and to ensure that all steps for mitigation as well as new risks are documented.

Now that we have discussed how to create a risk registry, we need to take a step back and talk more in depth about how we can identify gaps in coverage, test our current coverage, and how we can use any coverage gaps to fill in our risk registry.

Red and blue make purple – how to run purple team exercises

Purple teaming, as mentioned in *Chapter 1*, can be an important exercise in the SOC to test detections. On the other hand, it helps prove the negative or, in general, where risks can be identified. In this section, we're going to work through some possibilities for using purple team exercises and talk through some common open source tools that can be critically helpful in running successful purple teams.

The first step to setting up a purple team is identifying the purpose and scope. In some cases, the purpose could be to evaluate a new tool such as a SIEM tool or an EDR platform; in other cases, it could be to test the response to a potential incident, train new team members, or prove where your gaps are. This should be planned out in advance of any engagement with a red team engineer, or whoever will be conducting the red team portion of the engagement. The next step would be to determine what tools will be used to conduct an engagement, and what tests will be used. The tool that my team typically uses is **Atomic Red**, from Red Canary, and is an open source tool found at `https://github.com/redcanaryco/atomic-red-team`. One of the best parts of Atomic Red is that it is aligned with the MITRE ATT&CK Framework, which we will take a deeper dive into, starting in *Chapter 3, Reviewing Different Threat Models*. Here is an example of a test plan for a purple team exercise:

T1049: Systems Network Connection Discovery	
Atomic Test #1: Command Execution	2
Atomic Test #2: OS API Execution	1
Atomic Test #3: Process Creation	4
T1222.002 Linux and Mac File and Directory Permissions Modification	
Atomic Test #1: chmod - Change file or folder mode (numeric mode) [macos, linux]	3
Atomic Test #2: chmod - Change file or folder mode (symbolic mode) [macos, linux]	3
Atomic Test #3: chmod - Change file or folder mode (numeric mode) recursively [macos, linux]	4
Atomic Test #4: chmod - Change file or folder mode (symbolic mode) recursively [macos, linux]	3
Atomic Test #5: chown - Change file or folder ownership and group [macos, linux]	2
Atomic Test #6: chown - Change file or folder ownership and group recursively [macos, linux]	4
Atomic Test #7: chown - Change file or folder mode ownership only [macos, linux]	2
Atomic Test #8: chown - Change file or folder ownership recursively [macos, linux]	1
Atomic Test #9: chattr - Remove immutable file attribute [macos, linux]	3
Atomic Test #10: Chmod through c script [macos, linux]	2

Figure 2.2 – A purple team test plan

As you can see in the preceding figure, there is a **T number**, which is for the technique that is used while aligning with the ATT&CK framework, and each section's title. From there, it corresponds to the exact tests that were run and includes the results, which correspond with a number on the far right. The rating system was from 1 to 5:

1. The attack was identified and stopped by current security tools

2. The attack succeeded and was alerted on but was not stopped

3. The attack succeeded and generated events, but no alert was created

4. The attack was successful with no events or alerts

5. The attack failed due to incorrect commands

This type of plan allowed us to not only document what we were testing and the success of it but also check that the commands we were using from Atomic Red were correct. You can then take the findings from the plan and take screenshots of any successful attempts, as well as capture metrics on the efficiency of detections and tools. In *Figure 2.2*, we can see that of the 13 tests, 0 were rated 5, 3 were rated 4, 4 were rated 3, 4 were rated 5, and 2 were rated 1. Overall, I would say that the security posture for the organization in question needs work, but even though the outcome is negative, they now know where their gaps are and the plan to move forward.

The first instinct when seeing a report or plan such as the one in *Figure 2.2* could be to immediately think that you'll need an increase in budget and to obtain more or replace some security tools, but that might not necessarily be the case. The first step to mitigation could be to review your current policies and procedures. For example, in the cases where alerts were generated, you would want to create and maintain playbooks, which offer a step-by-step system for triaging alerts. For example, a playbook for a phishing alert might look like this:

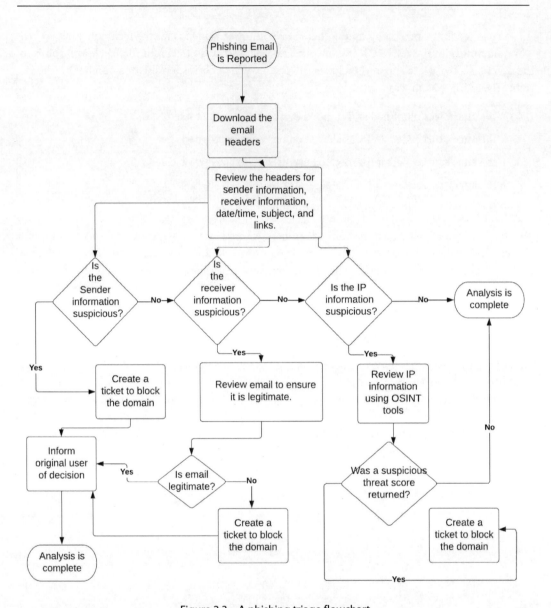

Figure 2.3 – A phishing triage flowchart

This playbook takes you from the time a phishing email is alerted to looking through the email headers and completing the analysis. Of course, this playbook would need to be specific to your environment, and you would want to include additional information, such as where the alert would be generated from, but it is a starting point. Any detection that is created should have a corresponding set of steps to triage to ensure there is continuity and scalability among your team. That alone would mean that any attack that generated an alert would be triaged, and throughout the purple team exercise, you can test out the triage steps to ensure that they are correct and make any changes necessary. Another mitigation step could be to just tune the tools that you are currently using. It's entirely possible that the tools might be misconfigured and, therefore, are not alerting as efficiently as they could. The other option would be to increase visibility either through setting up a network tap, reconfiguring the location of certain tools, or ingesting additional logs. In general, you should look to exhaust all options of mitigations rather than adding on additional tools, because if your foundation isn't strong, a new tool might help in the short term but will not be a long-term scalable solution. The best part about creating any mitigating steps is that you know how to test them as you can start by using the same plan and then evolving your purple team exercises to include additional techniques. As a rule of thumb, I recommend having some form of purple team exercise on a quarterly basis. This could be to test only a specific set of techniques or to test everything, but this means that you are reviewing your security posture on a quarterly basis and is a sign of a mature security team.

Purple team exercises are a critical part of any security program, especially the SOC. They provide a relatively cheap (the cost is resources) process to test out tools and processes, supply risks for the risk registry, train personnel, and educate them on current and real risks within your environment through presenting your report and evidence of the findings. The report should also include recommendations for improvements and identify any shortcomings in the environment. The next section discusses what some common coverage gaps are and security shortfalls and steps that can be taken to mitigate the situation.

Discussing common coverage gaps and security shortfalls

Security shortfalls and coverage gaps are similar to risk, in that they will always happen. The key is to find a way to work around the gaps and mitigate the situation as much as possible to help your organization mature. Additionally, we'll hear from an industry security practitioner on their experience and where their most common gaps are.

The most common gap I have seen is a lack of coverage due to a lack of logs being ingested. Security teams are in an odd position where they typically want to ingest as many logs as possible to have as much visibility as possible, even though you might not need all the logs all the time. In fact, most times, it'll be cost-prohibitive to ingest all your logs into a SIEM tool such as **Splunk** or **QRadar**, so you'll either have to prioritize what logs are ingested or have to use multiple different screens and tools, which makes it harder to correlate data. One way around this is to send logs to a data lake, which we could query and then ingest the detections and data on an ad hoc basis, but that relies on the expertise of the team or an additional tool. Another way to partially solve this is by utilizing integration to ingest alerts from other tools but not necessarily events. While this means that you still can't have a single pane of glass to look at all the correlated data in, you will at least be able to partially have it and can go to the other tools as needed. Having the correlated data will allow for a more complete view when triaging alerts, which could lead to a faster time to detect or a faster time to triage.

Another common gap would be user education. Security is a team effort for the entire company and is not restricted to the security team. A comprehensive training plan tests end users using phishing tests via tools such as **KnowBe4** or **GoPhish**. Those tests will allow you to gather metrics on the percentage of users that click on the phishing links and assign any users that click them resources to review or additional training. This allows you to create a more cyber-aware workforce.

A third area that is almost always a shortfall is that many organizations still operate as flat organizations. That means that the organization is all under one overarching security policy or group. In actuality, similar to systems, you want to identify who the high targets are, and then place them in a group with additional security procedures and additional monitoring. You also want to set up groups for the separate business units so that you can ensure privileged commands only from the expected groups and ensure that the principle of least privilege and separation of duties are intact.

In a recent conversation with Allen Ramsay, a current computer security analyst and former exploitation analyst, he mentioned that his common shortfall is identifying network traffic and having roughly normal traffic to compare for the purpose of assisting with threat-hunting. This brought up a good point because, in any aspect of security, you need to have an understanding of what normal looks like so you can identify suspicious traffic. Allen brought up the point that creating baselines for traffic and systems, sometimes referred to as a **golden image**, is key to ensuring that your organization understands what *normal* looks like, and that helps to quickly identify anomalous traffic.

One of the best ways to prepare and learn how to respond to gaps and coverage is through the use of **TTXs**. TTXs allow you to gather all stakeholders, who could be members of specific teams or only the security team; it really depends on the scenario. You then talk with the stakeholders about a hypothetical scenario and work through the scenario as if it were an active incident. This way, you can test to ensure that everyone understands their role in an incident but also identify gaps, which can be added to the risk register and eventually mitigated.

Gaps in coverage and shortfalls occur whenever you bring in a new system, stand up a new team, or, in general, they just happen. It's important for your team to actively review your shortfalls and gaps and ensure that they are documented as part of the risk registry.

Summary

This chapter covered how to create a risk registry and the format to use. As mentioned, a risk registry is not only critical for compliance purposes but also allows you to appropriately assess risk, track any changes in your organization, and ensure that you are making progress toward mitigating risks. We covered how to conduct a purple team exercise and showed a purple team report. Purple team exercises are a sign of a mature security program and are critical for implementing a trust-but-verify strategy in your security measures. The last position any incident responder wants to be in is responding to a critical incident that could have been mitigated or prevented if the team had just run a purple team exercise or a TTX and learned from those experiences. Finally, we covered some common gaps and shortcomings that are completely normal and discussed options for mitigating those gaps.

In the next chapter, we'll cover different threat models in detail and discuss how you can apply them to your environment.

3
Reviewing Different Threat Models

Threat modeling is a key component within any **security operation center** (**SOC**) and security environment as a whole, and just as with any SOC environment, there is no one size fits all for threat models.

This chapter will cover multiple threat models, their use cases, and their advantages and disadvantages. Doing so will allow the reader to apply the one that makes the most sense for their environment as well as provide a comparison point for comparing those threat models to ATT&CK:

- Reviewing the PASTA threat model and use cases
- Reviewing the STRIDE threat model and use cases
- Reviewing the VAST threat model and use cases
- Reviewing the Trike threat model and use cases
- Reviewing attack trees

Technical requirements

For this specific chapter, there are no installations or specific technologies that are required.

Reviewing the PASTA threat model and use cases

Threat modeling is a critical part of any SOC environment and team. It can be used as discussed to identify risks and gaps and for strategy, or it can be used for informational campaigns. Like all things, there are multiple different types of threat models, and there is no one size fits all for the types. The first threat model that we'll analyze and talk through use cases is the **Process for Attack Simulation and Threat Analysis** (**PASTA**) threat model. PASTA is a risk-centered threat model that combines risk analysis and the surrounding context into your risk mitigation and security strategy.

In development terms, thinks of PASTA as an incremental development process where you constantly go through cycles and make changes without having to start at the beginning of the model again. The main steps of the PASTA method are as follows:

1. **Define the objective**: This means setting the overall purpose for the threat model. This could be specific to a compliance framework or specific project in your organization.

2. **Identify the technical scope**: Once you have the overall objective, you need to identify the resources needed. You must identify what systems will be within scope and what personnel, if any, will be needed. Essentially, you want to outline anything needed to help ensure you can create a successful threat model. You also want to use this time to verify the scope and ensure you have the correct attack surface.

3. **Application decomposition**: In this stage, you take it one step further from having the scope, resources, and attack surface identified by producing the supporting documentation. This means that you produce data classification documents, data flow diagrams, and network diagrams, among other things. Essentially, you want to identify how all applications within scope are interconnected and where there are areas for connections, both inbound and outbound, that need to be assessed.

4. **Threat analysis**: In this stage, you want to ensure that you understand all the possible threats that face the applications, systems, and anything else within scope. You should document all possible threats to create a threat landscape document.

5. **Vulnerability analysis**: Here, you not only want to look at what your process is for identifying vulnerabilities but also identify any applicable vulnerabilities to the systems that are within scope and review or refine your process for remediating the vulnerabilities.

6. **Model potential attacks**: This stage works well with purple team exercises, which is where someone attempts attacks to test security procedures and responses. In a similar action, purple team attacks can help justify the threat and vulnerability analysis that you completed and let you know whether you have the correct analysis. You can also use this stage to create what are known as **attack trees**, which will be covered in the *Reviewing attack trees* section in this chapter.

7. **Complete a risk and impact analysis**: The final stage is for you to complete any reporting needed to review the impact of the threats identified and the modeled attacks so that you can assign an appropriate rating. Once you have your threat model completed, you can make a plan for mitigating or remediating any risks, or in some cases just accepting the risk.

The overall deliverable varies depending on what your organization wants, so it might be a chart such as a tree structure, it might be in an Excel sheet, or it might even be in the form of a presentation that is linked to tickets for tracking. In whatever form it is in, it must be reviewed on a regular basis to ensure that it is accurate and up-to-date with any system changes.

The benefits of using the PASTA threat model as opposed to others is that it is a thorough process of identifying the scope, reviewing all systems and processes, validating through technical and non-technical means, and completing a comprehensive report in the form of a risk profile, which details high-level risks with an overall risk score, and can show more in-depth data if needed. A possible application risk profile page could look something like this:

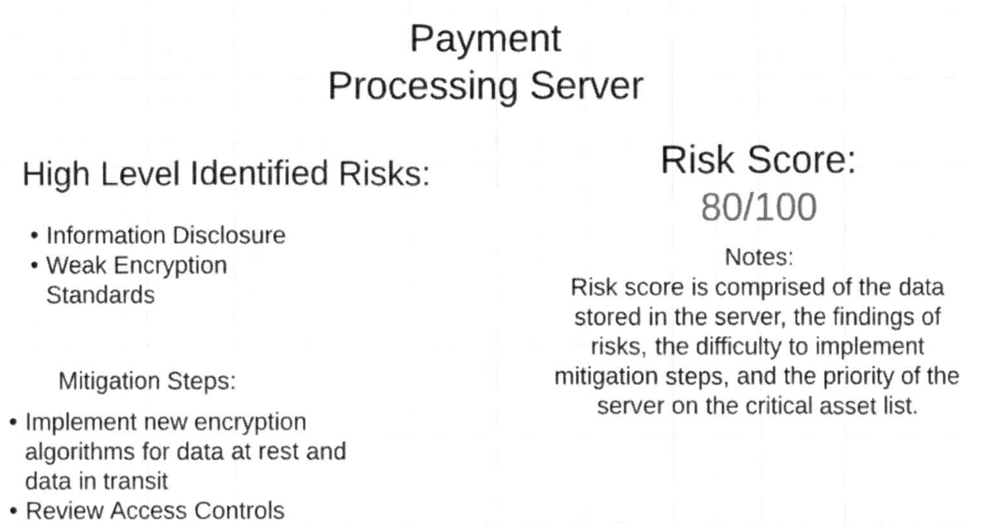

Payment Processing Server

High Level Identified Risks:

- Information Disclosure
- Weak Encryption Standards

Mitigation Steps:

- Implement new encryption algorithms for data at rest and data in transit
- Review Access Controls

Risk Score:
80/100

Notes:
Risk score is comprised of the data stored in the server, the findings of risks, the difficulty to implement mitigation steps, and the priority of the server on the critical asset list.

Figure 3.1 – Simple application risk report

In the preceding screenshot, you see a very simplified application risk report, which lists the high-level risks, the overall risk scoring, the application, and the recommended mitigation steps. It is recommended to include something like the preceding screenshot for a briefing; however, you would want to create an in-depth report that shows the methodology used, the steps taken to analyze the threats and vulnerabilities, the full list of vulnerabilities and threats with proof and scoring where applicable, and a full list of recommendations. If possible, you would also want to identify the risk owners or name the teams responsible for changes to the application that is being analyzed.

In this section, we covered the PASTA threat model and its steps. The PASTA threat model is one type of threat model that is commonly used for identifying and modeling threats so that they can be rated and monitored regularly. The PASTA threat model is primarily used in cases where you want to identify gaps, create informational campaigns, or help guide your organizational cyber strategy. It is used on more of a scope basis instead of being an organization-wide option. In the next section, we'll look at the STRIDE threat model, which differs because it is primarily used in development environments.

Reviewing the STRIDE threat model and use cases

The **Spoofing, Tampering, Repudiation, Information Disclosure, Denial of Service, and Elevation of Privilege (STRIDE)** threat model is unique in that it is primarily used for development environments and, for a while, was known for being synonymous with Microsoft because it was created by two Microsoft employees, Loren Kohnfelder and Praerit Garg. Each of the six categories in this model can be correlated to a core security concept that the authors tried to focus on. The concepts are like the **confidentiality, integrity, and availability (CIA)** triad.

The CIA triad is used to guide security policies and guidelines based on what is more important in your organization. This simple model is the basis for all security in that it provides a core focus for making security decisions based on how you value those three principles. Confidentiality is the principle of keeping data and systems private and can be linked to items like the principle of least privilege and access control in general and it plays a role in encryption to ensure data is not intercepted. Integrity is the idea that all information is kept in its intended form and not altered. That means that any data reviewed can be trusted. Integrity can be accomplished through implementing digital signatures on the information. Availability means that all systems, services, and data are accessible. One technical control that can help maintain availability is by having comprehensive backups, which systems can be restored from in the case of an outage. In the security field, you use the CIA triad for classifying where vulnerabilities fall and what principles they would impact, on prioritization of efforts, and, as mentioned, to guide decisions. Essentially, when reviewing, you would want to devise a rating system to determine which out of the three principles is the most important in that case, and your actions should follow that. In a perfect world, of course, all principles would be balanced, but again it all depends on your use case. The CIA triad would look like this, with the dot representing the principles you would lean into. In the case of the following diagram, we can see that we prioritize integrity and availability over confidentiality:

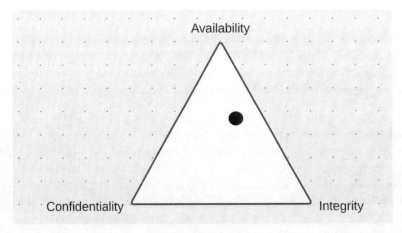

Figure 3.2 – CIA triad

As stated, the CIA triad is the basis for all security decisions, and that includes the categories for the STRIDE threat model. The CIA triad concepts that correlate to the six categories are as follows:

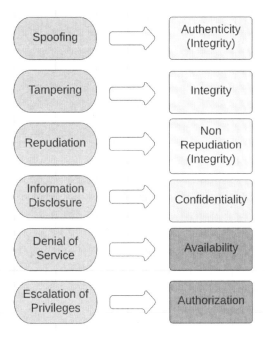

Figure 3.3 – STRIDE correlated to the corresponding CIA triad attributes

The green boxes are color-coordinated for integrity, the orange box for confidentiality, and the red boxes for availability.

In addition to understanding the CIA triad properties, you'll want an understanding of the potential threats and meanings for each of the individual categories. They are as follows:

- **Spoofing**: This is an attack or method where the malicious actor masks their identity by displaying a fake name, email, URL, and so on. It is done to trick the unsuspecting user into clicking on or responding to something that they believe is legitimate when it is not. Spoofing is commonly performed by phishing emails.

- **Tampering**: This includes modifying a system or data without authorization. An example of tampering can be a *man-in-the-middle attack*.

- **Repudiation**: This is when a system does not have proper audit logging or audit logs have been tampered with by deletion or editing. Repudiation issues occur when a malicious action is taken, and steps are taken to cover the tracks.

- **Information disclosure**: While information disclosure can be intentional, in this case, the model is concerned with unintentional information disclosure. That can be done through attacks such as data exfiltration or unauthorized access, which would allow data harvesting.

- **Denial of service**: A **denial-of-service (DOS)** or **distributed denial-of-service (DDoS)** attack occurs when actions or requests are sent to the receiving system at a rate that overwhelms the system or service and renders it unusable for other users. An example of a DOS or DDoS attack would be a botnet attack or a SYN flood.

- **Escalation of privileges**: Similar to information disclosure, privileges can be escalated through intentional means; however, unintentional or unauthorized escalation of privileges can lead to the installation of malware and information disclosure and violates the principle of least privilege, among other types of attacks.

You might be wondering, at this point, why this threat model is primarily used with development environments. The reason for that is that the STRIDE model has specific categories to make it easy to fit within the development life cycle methodologies and is used primarily to find flaws or shortcomings in apps with a security-by-design approach. It can also be easily diagramed, as the following example shows, and can be linked to other controls such as those in the **National Institute of Standards and Technology (NIST) Risk Management Framework (RMF)** standards, which are used for federal compliance. A simple example of the STRIDE model would look like this:

System	Category	Impact	Risk Rating	Mitigating Factors	Remediation Steps	Related Controls
Card Reader Software v 1.2	Tampering	Change the routing information for card data	8	Access Controls	Implement Validation Checks for all Changes	RMF:SA-18
Card Reader Software v 1.2	Escalation of Privileges	Allow for unauthorized access	3	Enforce Session Timeouts	Securely code access controls	RMF:AC-6, AC-3
Card Reader Software v 1.2	Denial of Service	Brick the system to not allow requests	5	Implement Load Balancing	Implement rate limits	
Card Reader Software v 1.2	Information Disclosure	Disclosure of PCI data.	7	Data Encryption	Review Encryption standards are secure enough	

Table 3.1 – A simple example of how the STRIDE model can be recorded

The STRIDE model, as mentioned, was developed by Microsoft and used primarily in the design phase and in development environments. Since it is part of the design phase, this approach is an example of proactive security rather than reactive. That also provides benefits in the concept of security by design, so it can be easy to implement in the planning stages. One of the downsides to the STRIDE model is that the six categories can be limited in how you categorize risks and can be less thorough than the PASTA model.

In this section, we covered what the STRIDE model is, what the categories are, what the categories relate to, and a little bit about the CIA Triad. We also learned what some of the benefits of the STRIDE model are and what one of its weaknesses is. The next model we'll cover is the VAST threat model, as well as others, to be able to compare the different models.

Reviewing the VAST threat model and use cases

The **Visual, Agile, and Simple Threat** (**VAST**) threat model is an approach that casts a wide net, as the word **vast** suggests. It's a threat model that attempts to look at all possible threats in all scenarios and, as we may imagine, it can be a daunting task to take on. The basis of this model, similar to other models, is based on an open source threat analysis tool, in this case, called **ThreatModeler**. In the case of the VAST model, you use a data flow diagram for the organization as well as an organizational flow diagram to identify any operational threats. One of the benefits of the VAST model is that it addresses operational risks, whereas some of the other models do not. Another benefit of this model is that it is far-reaching, so you can look at an organization as a whole and both technical and non-technical components to complete the threat model. Some of the downsides of the VAST threat model are that it can be overwhelming, depending on the organization size and scope size, to include both technical and non-technical options, which can lead to missing potential threats based on the resources dedicated to analyzing the model. One of the ways to mitigate this is to attempt to implement the VAST model in the design phase, but that can lead to having to make changes due to operational changes and data flow changes, which frequently occur in the development process. This risk can also lead to an incomplete model. The other option is to automate as much as possible, which is why tools such as ThreatModeler are so important.

Using tools to automate can definitely save time. Most of those types of tools will analyze the data flow diagram and other user input and identify the risks based on the data provided. The main positive of this approach is that you save time and can generate new threat models regularly. One of the downsides is that if you do not input the correct data and forget to change it, then you have an inaccurate threat model, which could lead you to make incorrect strategical decisions or use resources to focus on mitigations based on inaccurate prioritizations. The other downside to analyzing risks is that the diagram risks might be different in reality, and you would be able to validate those risks with threat analysis and modeling. An example of a threat model using the VAST approach is shown here:

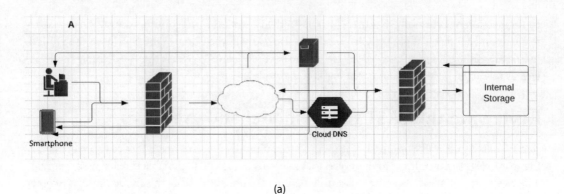

(a)

(b)

Figure 3.4 – Operational and technical data flow

As you can see from the preceding diagrams, there is an operational data flow diagram, *(a)*, which shows the users from computers and phones requesting to access the file server and public-facing DNS, and then we have additional connections and details to show the technical information *(b)*. The point is with VAST, you need to capture both levels, and in a real situation, you would want to include as much information as possible to automate the identification of risks.

Now we know what the VAST threat model is and some of its benefits and downsides. Personally, I've used plenty of threat modeling automation tools and think they can be very helpful in getting started with the threat models for your organization. The key is to make sure that you validate any findings. Next, we are going to cover the TRIKE threat model, and some use cases.

Reviewing the Trike threat model and use cases

The Trike threat model is focused on the objective of threat modeling from a risk standpoint. This type of threat model is typically paired with risk registries so that it can be targeted to the specific risks and needs that you perceive. Most of the time, these threat models are tied to auditing or compliance requirements, and they are based on the specific requirements of the organization. It combines those requirements with risk owners and establishes the level of acceptable risk. It differs from the PASTA and STRIDE models because it is a risk-based approach instead of utilizing the systems and attack approach of the other models. The point of this model is to accomplish the following:

- Communicate what the risks are within the organization
- Determine the acceptable risk threshold with input from all stakeholders for the organization
- Establish the risk owners for the applicable risks, to be held accountable for mitigations and failures
- Allow all applicable risk owners and teams to understand the risks for the organization and to make recommendations for reducing the risks

The steps to completing the threat model in an effective form are to first establish what the requirements are, and that can vary depending on the business mission, compliance requirements, or other internal priorities. Then, you need to create a data flow document, which shows all aspects of the organization and how requests and traffic move throughout the organization. From there, you can identify what the threats are, assign risks, and assign owners. An example of a data flow diagram is the following:

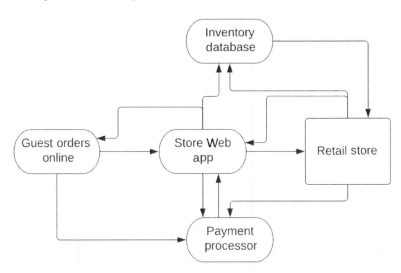

Figure 3.5 – Simple data flow diagram to build the TRIKE threat model

The simple data flow diagram shows a user going to a store's page, placing an order, the order using the payment processor and the database to query for inventory, and reaching out to the retail store and then back to the guest. Of course, in actuality, this diagram would be larger and more complex but, even from this small diagram, we can build a basic TRIKE threat model from the risk associated with the payment processor connections and the connections to the database. A potential Trike threat model from the diagram would look like this:

Requirement	Risk Concern	Risk Rating	Risk Owner	Priority	Notes:
Encrypted calls to the payment processor	Data would be succeptible to a Man-In-The-Midde attack	8	CTO	High	PCI-DSS Compliance
Data sanitization in the inventory database	Database would be succeptible to an injection attack	6	CTO	Moderate	Risk Management Framework
Fraudulent charge protection	Fraudulent cards and payments would be accepted and cause a PCI-DSS	9	CISO	High	PCI-DSS Compliance

Table 3.2 – Trike threat model based on the data flow diagram

As you can see in the preceding table, we have identified some areas of concern and requirements, listed risk ratings, identified a risk owner, prioritized the risks, and added notes, which in this case, correlates to the compliance framework that the requirements come from. The benefit to using this approach is that it is very logical in that you already have the established requirements from other sources; however, it can be limiting. For instance, for the PASTA threat model, where you analyze risks and vulnerabilities through means such as purple team exercises, the Trike threat model can potentially miss risks because it might not be listed in the initial set of requirements.

The TRIKE model is very important for organizations that know their requirements and are used in use cases that are for preparation for audits. This clearly varies from the PASTA, STRIDE, and VAST threat models, and there are clear pros and cons to both options. The next topic covered is attack trees, which can be used in conjunction with any threat model or on their own.

Reviewing attack trees

As with all threat models, there are visual representations that coincide with the respective threat models, and attack trees are no different. An attack tree is a logical and step-based way to represent a threat and how it would affect an organization or system. It starts with the initial vector; for example, a phishing email is received, and an employee falls for the malicious email. The next level of the tree shows the possible outcomes; so, in this case, one branch could be for the malicious user to gain access to the system or account. Another branch could be that credentials are compromised, and it would continue from there. If we wanted to see an example of a simple phishing attack tree from a risk perspective, it would look like this:

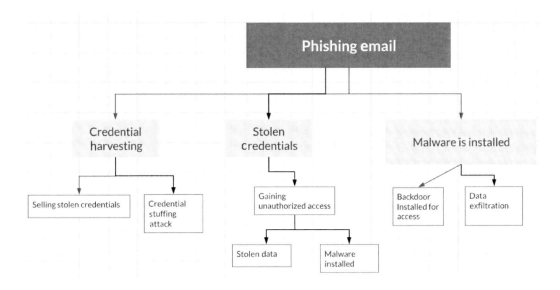

Figure 3.6 – Simple phishing risks attack chart

Again, the preceding example is strictly based around documenting risks, whereas you can also use attack trees to document how the attacks would happen, which could be useful in cases where you need to explain what the potential tasks are and get your point across on how they are conducted to implement effective protections. An example from the *how* perspective of a phishing attack might look like this:

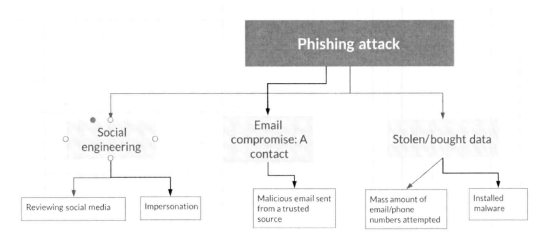

Figure 3.7 – Simple attack map from the perspective of how phishing could occur

As you can see from the two diagrams, both are versions of attack maps; however, they greatly differ in their purpose. The diagram in *Figure 3.6* shows the possible risks of a successful threat model, whereas the diagram in *Figure 3.7* shows the possible ways that a phishing attack could occur. Both diagrams are useful and can be used to show the methodology behind threats and attacks as well as allow you to address all possible outcomes of an attack with mitigation steps to ensure your organization is protected.

One of the large positives of attack trees is that they are used frequently and can be used in conjunction with any threat models or on their own. Attack trees are also frequently used in security tools, so your analysts have likely had exposure to them already. One downside is that when creating them from scratch, they can be timely, and it's possible to miss use cases and causes of attacks, but if done correctly, these types of documents can be used with playbooks and runbooks, which help with training analysts, identifying risks, and making your team more scalable.

Attack trees are one of the original threat models and are still regularly used today. They are clearly very different from the other threat models in that they don't necessarily need requirements to be identified, an in-depth scope, or automation. However, they can be used to identify all types of attacks and work through the risks and modifications. As mentioned, they can also be used as an appendix item for any threat model, and it's recommended that you do so.

Summary

In this chapter, we reviewed the PASTA, STRIDE, VAST, and Trike threat models as well as attack trees from both a risk- and attack-identification perspective. Throughout your career, you will use a combination of the threat models discussed, or even others, to find the best combination to fit your organization because, like most things, there is no true "one size fits all" for threat models. Threat models are also a concept that you want to be comfortable with because they are a constant task; whether it's creating the initial models or validating them to ensure they are still accurate; threat models are constantly changing. For a quick reference on the different models, use this chart:

PASTA threat model	STRIDE threat model	VAST threat model	Trike threat model	Attack trees
Seven-step framework approach Risk-centric Allows for a very in-depth approach	Primarily used in Microsoft environments	Casts a wide net Based on a threat modeler tool result	Used for communicating risk between all organizational system owners	The original threat model Can be created for each individual attack vector

Table 3.3 – A quick reference on the models covered

In the next chapter, we'll start looking at the MITRE ATT&CK framework, which is commonly used in the security industry to align threats, attacks, and mitigation strategies.

4
What Is the ATT&CK Framework?

This chapter will outline the evolution of the ATT&CK Framework and the various different high-level configurations for types of systems (i.e., cloud, mobile, Windows, etc.). It will also be the first introduction to related use cases. We will cover the following topics:

- A brief history and evolution of ATT&CK

- Overview of the various ATT&CK models

A brief history and evolution of ATT&CK

The ATT&CK Framework is obviously the main portion of the book, so let's start with the basics and learn about the history, purpose, categories, and overview of different models within this chapter.

The MITRE ATT&CK Framework was founded in 2015. It started off as a total of 9 tactics and 96 techniques and quickly gained traction for how threats and attacks were categorized and organized in security. It currently stands at version 11, released in April 2022, which has 14 tactics, 191 techniques, 386 sub-techniques, and 134 groups, and covers 680 pieces of software. It remains one of the top comprehensive knowledge bases out there. Over the years, it has included specific operating systems and different types of infrastructures and environments, making it a more practical framework for categorizing threats against your environment as a whole. The growth from 2015 to 2022 alone shows the amount of work that has gone into identifying new techniques, detections, and mitigation strategies, and it has continued to be publicly accessible for everyone to use as a resource when evaluating their environments. The matrices continue to be tweaked and perfected and new matrices are being added. According to the release notes from version 11 of ATT&CK, **ATT&CK for Mobile** is still in beta, which shows future plans for advancement and continued development. They also list out all of the techniques and sub-techniques that have changed in the update and list out new techniques that have been added, so you can quickly digest the new information without having to dig through the matrices by yourself.

All of the matrices are to be used as a guideline when evaluating and categorizing risks and techniques. In fact, a large portion of security tools now align detections with MITRE ATT&CK, and it continues to gain more popularity as a resource, strategy, and now even a certification with Certified MITRE ATT&CK Defender, which covers *Fundamentals*, *Cyber Threat Intelligence*, *Security Operations Center Assessments*, *Adversary Emulation Methodology*, and *Threat Hunting Detection Engineering*, but more are sure to be created in the future. This means that understanding the framework is a valuable skill for any cyber practitioner, and you should have both theoretical knowledge and practical knowledge, meaning you not only understand what the techniques are but also how to create an implementation and categorize threats in your network to align with the framework.

The continued evolution of the matrices means that this is a tool in and of itself in addition to being a resource that is integrated with many of the current cybersecurity tools. This is used to build justification for monitoring, more mature detection, and justification for implementing mitigations. It can even be used to associate criticality with different techniques based on your environment, which gives you a prioritization system so you can focus your efforts on the areas that need the most help.

Understanding the history of models allows you to appreciate the work that has gone in from countless folks to develop a strategic tool that is used by thousands of people every year. The MITRE ATT&CK Framework is only going to continue to advance, grow, and be more applicable to more environments, so it's important to be able to learn and speak about it and apply controls effectively. The next section will cover a brief overview of the current ATT&CK model, including the tactics, matrices, and a small sampling of examples of techniques and sub-techniques.

Overview of the various ATT&CK models

As mentioned, the MITRE ATT&CK Framework has evolved to include multiple different models based on operating systems and environments. Currently, these are the following models:

- Windows
- macOS
- Linux
- Network
- Containers
- Office 365
- Azure AD
- Google Workspaces
- **Software as a Service (SaaS)**
- **Infrastructure as a Service (IaaS)**

- Android

- iOS

- **Industrial Control System (ICS)**

These models are meant to be used in a pick-and-choose manner so that, as an end user, you are able to select the techniques and matrices that apply to your environment and mix and match options as needed. We'll take a deep-dive into quite a few of the different models by looking at the types of techniques and comparison of the different models through future chapters. However, from a basic point of view, they are all initially based on a version of the **Cyber Kill Chain** framework. The Cyber Kill Chain framework, developed by Lockheed Martin, involves the following stages:

1. **Reconnaissance** – Used for information gathering, scanning, and so on.

2. **Weaponization** – An attacker will choose an exploit based on the information gathered in the reconnaissance phase and package the exploit for the next stage.

3. **Delivery** – The exploit that was packaged during the weaponization phase is sent to the potential victim. Methods to send the package include phishing, whaling, drive-by download, and so on.

4. **Exploitation** – The exploit that was weaponized and delivered in previous stages has now been executed on the victim's account/system.

5. **Installation** – The malware/exploit has been installed and detonated on the victim's system or account and is considered an active infection at this point.

6. **Command and control** – Due to this being an active infection, the malware or exploit will have established persistent communications in multiple different forms. One possible form would be through a periodic beacon, which essentially sends network traffic from the infected host to a C2 server to let the attacker know what systems are still compromised.

7. **Action on objectives** – The exploit or malware has completed its objective, which could be something such as exfiltration of data, opening a backdoor, logging keystrokes, and so on.

> **Note**
> There are other simplified versions of the Cyber Kill Chain that various companies have created and implemented within their products, but the Lockheed Martin one is the original.

The Cyber Kill Chain stages are also broken into more granular tactics:

1. Reconnaissance: Reconnaissance

2. Resource Development: Weaponization

3. Initial Access: Exploitation

4. Execution: Delivery

5. Persistence: Command and Control

6. Privilege Escalation: Installation

7. Defense Evasion: Installation

8. Credential Access: Exploitation

9. Discovery: Reconnaissance

10. Lateral Movement: Exploitation

11. Collection: Actions on Objectives

12. Command and Control: Command and Control

13. Exfiltration: Actions on Objectives

14. Impact: Actions on Objectives

After the tactics, they are broken into techniques and sub-techniques. Some examples of techniques are **Hijack Execution Flow**, **File and Directory Permissions Modification**, and **Forge Web Credentials**. They can be broken down as follows:

Stage	Persistence	Defense Evasion	Credential Access
Technique Number	T1574	T1222	T1606
Title	Hijack Execution Flow	File and Directory Permissions Modification	Forge Web Credentials
Description	This is the process of a malicious user potentially hijacking the way operating systems run programs and using that to execute their malicious payloads.	Malicious Users can modify access lists to evade detection and maintain persistence.	Malicious Users have the ability to forge credentials to use to gain access to web applications.
Sub Techniques	DLL Search Order Hijacking, DLL Side-Loading, Dylib Hijacking, Executable Installer File Permissions Weakness, Dynamic Linker Hijacking, Path Interception by PATH Environment Variable, Pather Interception by Search Order Hijacking, Path Interception by Unquoted Path, Services File Permissions Weakness, Services Registy Permissions Weakness, COR_PROFILER, KernelCallbackTable	Windows File and Directory Permissions Modification, Linux and Mac File and Directory Permissions Modification	Web Cookies, SAML Tokens
References	https://attack.mitre.org/techniques/T1574/	https://attack.mitre.org/techniques/T	https://attack.mitre.org/techniques/T1606/
Other Tactics	Privilege Escalation, Defense Evasion		

Figure 4.1 – MITRE ATT&CK examples

As we can see from the preceding chart, we have the category, which is also a **tactic**. Next, we have the **technique number**. Every technique within the matrices has its own unique number, and all sub-techniques have the an identification number with **.001**, so for example, the sub-technique of **DLL Search Order Hijacking** would have the technique number **T1574.001**. Then, there is a **description**, but to get that, you would have to select the technique you were interested in within the matrices and go to the reference link. On In the matrix itself, it does show all of the sub-techniques:

Defense Evasion

42 techniques

Abuse Elevation Control Mechanism (4)	
Access Token Manipulation (5)	
BITS Jobs	
Build Image on Host	
Debugger Evasion	
Deobfuscate/Decode Files or Information	
Deploy Container	
Direct Volume Access	
Domain Policy Modification (2)	
Execution Guardrails (1)	
Exploitation for Defense Evasion	
File and Directory Permissions Modification (2)	Windows File and Directory Permissions Modification
	Linux and Mac File and Directory Permissions Modification
Hide Artifacts (10)	

(a)

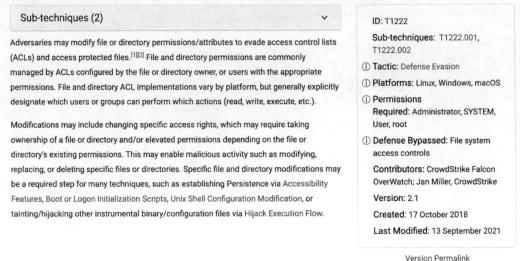

File and Directory Permissions Modification

Sub-techniques (2)   ⌄

Adversaries may modify file or directory permissions/attributes to evade access control lists (ACLs) and access protected files.[1][2] File and directory permissions are commonly managed by ACLs configured by the file or directory owner, or users with the appropriate permissions. File and directory ACL implementations vary by platform, but generally explicitly designate which users or groups can perform which actions (read, write, execute, etc.).

Modifications may include changing specific access rights, which may require taking ownership of a file or directory and/or elevated permissions depending on the file or directory's existing permissions. This may enable malicious activity such as modifying, replacing, or deleting specific files or directories. Specific file and directory modifications may be a required step for many techniques, such as establishing Persistence via Accessibility Features, Boot or Logon Initialization Scripts, Unix Shell Configuration Modification, or tainting/hijacking other instrumental binary/configuration files via Hijack Execution Flow.

ID: T1222

Sub-techniques: T1222.001, T1222.002

ⓘ **Tactic:** Defense Evasion

ⓘ **Platforms:** Linux, Windows, macOS

ⓘ **Permissions Required:** Administrator, SYSTEM, User, root

ⓘ **Defense Bypassed:** File system access controls

Contributors: CrowdStrike Falcon OverWatch; Jan Miller, CrowdStrike

Version: 2.1

Created: 17 October 2018

Last Modified: 13 September 2021

Version Permalink

Mitigations

(b)

Figure 4.2 – Screenshots from the MITRE ATT&CK Framework to show how data is represented

On the *reference* page, as mentioned, you get the description, any other tactics that the technique can be a part of (a technique can be in multiple different tactics but doesn't have to be), possible mitigation steps to lessen the risk of the technique, possible detection strategies, and additional resources specific to that technique. The reference pages for all techniques can be incredibly informative and helpful when learning about techniques and risk and learning how to apply risk categorizations to your organization.

One thing to keep in mind is that with the example and the matrix alone, while a lot of tactics or stages are the same as the ones listed in the Cyber Kill Chain, it's important to understand what the Cyber Kill Chain is and its purpose, as there are a few key differences between the two. The first difference is that the MITRE Framework is more detail-oriented than the Cyber Kill Chain. For example, the Cyber Kill Chain only has the overall tactics or stages listed and not techniques, sub-techniques, detections, mitigations, and so on. The second difference is that the Cyber Kill Chain is flat and does not have variable forms for different types of environments. This means that it attempts to take a one-stage-fits-all approach, and that's also why it must be more generalized than specific.

Another important aspect to remember is that not everything from the MITRE ATT&CK Framework can be implemented; for example, some techniques rely on you predicting the future for new malware, and while you want to try to predict what is coming next, you'll never be able to fully predict the future. That can be a downfall to being specific; the techniques or sub-techniques don't always fit, which is why it's important with the matrices to use them as a guide and apply concepts where needed. It's not a compliance framework where you are trying to obtain 100% of a matrix, and if you are taking that approach right now, you should stop and re-evaluate. Taking that approach will only lead to headaches and disappointment, so it's critical to analyze your environment and understand how to implement detection, mitigations, and controls that make sense within your environment and add value.

Summary

The MITRE ATT&CK Framework is important to understand and have as part of your foundation of information for a career in information security. The building blocks, such as how the matrices are used, how to build detections ranging from novice to expert in the depth of understanding, and learning new techniques due to the continued evolution of the matrices, keep you current in this industry.

In the next chapter, we'll begin our first of multiple deep-dives by looking at the enterprise-level matrices. We'll cover a large sampling of techniques, sub-techniques, detections, and mitigations. We'll also talk through real-world examples of implementing those detections and mitigations and the risks that can be associated with those techniques if they were to be exploited.

Part 2 – Detection Improvements and Alignment with ATT&CK

The second part of this book starts with a text-heavy chapter listing out the different tactics and techniques for a number of different MITRE ATT&CK framework matrices. Then, a few techniques are looked at further from each matrix. After the details of the framework are provided, the following chapter covers the practical knowledge of the framework so that you will be able to understand the matrices and apply mitigations and detections that can directly map to different techniques. This chapter also explores different detections that have a proven track record for working and covers some mistakes that are commonly made so that you may hopefully learn from them. This sets you up for the third part, which is focused on triaging the detections that have now been put in place.

This part has the following chapters:

- *Chapter 5, A Deep Dive into the ATT&CK Framework*
- *Chapter 6, Strategies to Map to ATT&CK*
- *Chapter 7, Common Mistakes with Implementation*
- *Chapter 8, Return on Investment Detections*

5

A Deep Dive into
the ATT&CK Framework

This chapter will provide a deeper look at the different techniques that are covered by the ATT&CK framework and the potential gaps in it. The reader will understand how to rank different techniques and their applicability to their own environments. This will focus specifically on the cloud, Windows, macOS, mobile, and network frameworks. We will cover the following topics:

- A deep dive into the techniques in the cloud framework

- A deep dive into the techniques in the Windows framework

- A deep dive into the techniques in the macOS framework

- A deep dive into the techniques in the network framework

- A deep dive into the techniques in the mobile framework

Technical requirements

For this specific chapter, there are no installations or specific technologies that are required.

A deep dive into the techniques in the cloud framework

As mentioned in *Chapter 4*, *What Is the ATT&CK Framework?*, the MITRE ATT&CK framework has different matrices for the different enterprises, one of those enterprises being the cloud. While this is great, you have to remember that you might have to customize any techniques so that they fit your specific cloud environment, but there are currently matrices for Office 365, Azure AD, Google Workspace, **Software as a Service (SaaS)**, and **Infrastructure as a Service (IaaS)**. In this section, we will start by looking at the tactics that are covered and the unique techniques before discussing the sub-techniques and supplemental information.

We'll start at the top by discussing the generic cloud enterprise matrix, which has the following tactics and techniques:

- Initial Access

  - Drive-by Compromise, Exploit Public Facing Application, Phishing, Trusted Relationship, and Valid Accounts

- Execution

  - User Execution and Serverless Execution

- Persistence

  - Account Manipulation, Create Account, Implant Internal Image, Office Application Startup, and Valid Accounts

- Privilege Escalation

  - Domain Policy Modification and Valid Accounts

- Defense Evasion

  - Domain Policy Modification, Hide Artifacts, Impair Defenses, Modify Cloud Compute Infrastructure, Unused/Unsupported Cloud Regions, Use Alternate Authentication Material, and Valid Accounts

- Credential Access

  - Brute Force, Forge Web Credentials, Multi-Factor Authentication Request Generation, Network Sniffing, Steal Application Access Token, Steal Web Session Cookie, and Unsecured Credentials

- Discovery

  - Account Discovery, Cloud Infrastructure Discovery, Cloud Service Dashboard, Cloud Service Discovery, Cloud Storage Object Discovery, Network Service Discovery, Network Sniffing, Password Policy Discovery, Permission Groups Discovery, Software Discovery, System Information Discovery, System Location Discovery, and System Network Connections Discovery

- Lateral Movement

  - Internal Spearphishing, Taint Shared Content, and Use Alternate Authentication Material

- Collection

  - Automated Collection, Data from Cloud Storage, Data from Information Repositories, Data Staged, and Email Collection

- Exfiltration:

  - Transfer Data to Cloud Account

- Impact:

  - Account Access Removal, Data Destruction, Data Encrypted for Impact, Defacement, Endpoint **Denial of Service** (**DoS**), Network Denial of Service, and Resource Hijacking

From looking at the generic cloud matrix, there are a few observations. The first observation is that not all tactics that are listed as possible options in *Chapter 4* are used. That shows that the tactics listed in each matrix might vary slightly depending on the applicability to the infrastructure that is being examined. The second observation is that there are some techniques that fall into multiple tactics; for example, you can see that Valid Accounts is in Initial Access, Persistence, Privilege Escalation, and Defense Evasion, which shows that techniques can have a one-to-many relationship with tactics. When in the matrix, you can take a deeper look and show sub-techniques and subsequent details. For example, in the technique of Account Manipulation under the Persistence tactic, there are five sub-techniques. The five sub-techniques are as follows:

- *Additional Cloud Credentials*: This can occur when an attacker creates or adds accounts to be able to maintain persistence.

- *Additional Email Delegate Permissions*: This occurs when an attacker grants themselves or delegates folder or mailbox privileges, which can be used to maintain persistence or for business email compromise.

- *Additional Cloud Roles*: This is where an attacker adds user roles in an order to maintain persistence or assign the role to a compromised user to elevate privileges.

- *Secure Shell Authorized Keys*: **Secure Shell** (**SSH**) is a network protocol used for encrypting network traffic over unsecured networks. For example, when a URL has an S at the end of HTTP (as in HTTPS), this means that the traffic to that site is encrypted, whereas http means that the traffic is unencrypted. This sub-technique is where an attacker would either compromise legitimate SSH-Authorized Keys or add new SSH Keys to maintain persistence and have possible root access.

- *Device Registration*: This is where an attacker would add a device to comply with an organization's MFA protocol and help maintain access.

Then, in the details of the technique and sub-technique, you are provided with a detailed description of the technique, procedure examples, mitigation, detection, and references. In this case, **Account Manipulation** is when a malicious user modifies credentials, roles, and so on in order to potentially elevate their privileges or carry out other nefarious activities. In this case, the attacker must already have some level of access to conduct an attack, such as social engineering, to gain access to a legitimate account.

Procedural examples are cases where known hacker groups have used these techniques in one of their hacks, and for this technique, one example is that APT3 has used account modification to add accounts to the local admin groups so that they have root-level privileges. APT3 is a China-based **Advanced Persistent Threat (APT)** group. APT groups are sophisticated, typically state-sponsored hacker groups.

Some steps that can be taken to mitigate the risk of account modification are to enable MFA and implement Privileged account management to ensure that only members that absolutely need admin privileges have it; essentially, it's implementing the **principle of least privilege**. Some methods for monitoring would be to monitor the log files on file modification, such as the `authorized_keys` file, for each use or monitoring locations for logins and accepted MFA pushes.

After looking at the generic cloud matrix, we can look at the Office 365 matrix. Office 365 has over 345 million paid users, so naturally, it is a popular tool, which makes it a popular target for hacker groups; this is why you would want to ensure monitoring is put in place that aligns with the matrix. Of course, Office 365 is a line-of-business tool package from Microsoft, which includes Outlook and Microsoft Word and is used online to allow work to be conducted in a collaborative manner and is a SaaS offering. The matrices for Office 365 cover the following tactics:

- Initial Access

  - Phishing and Valid Accounts

- Persistence

  - Account Manipulation, Create Account, Office Application Startup, and Valid Accounts

- Privilege Escalation

  - Valid Accounts

- Defense Evasion

  - Hide Artifacts, Impair Defenses, Use Alternate Authentication Material, and Valid Accounts

- Credential Access

  - Brute Force, Forge Web Credentials, Multi-Factor Authentication Request Generation, Steal Application Access Token, Steal Web Session Cookie, and Unsecured Credentials

- Discovery

  - Account Discovery, Cloud Service Dashboard, Cloud Service Discovery, Permission Groups Discovery, and Software Discovery

- Lateral Movement

  - Internal Spearphishing, Taint Shared Content, and Use Alternate Authentication Material

- Collection

  - Data from Information Repositories and Email Collection

- Impact

  - Account Access Removal, Endpoint Denial of Service, and Network Denial of Service

As you can see from the Office 365 matrix, it has far fewer techniques than the generic cloud matrix, because it is specific to Office 365. If we were to analyze one specific technique in this matrix, we could start with Office Application Startup in the Persistence tactic. We chose that technique because it will only show up on the Office 365 board and none of the other specific cloud boards; of course, it will show on the generic cloud matrix, because that matrix has all techniques across all of the specified matrices. The Office Application Startup technique contains six sub-techniques:

- *Office Template Macros*: **Macros** are small packages of code that are used to carry out an action. An attacker can add a malicious macro or inject code into an existing macro to obtain or maintain persistence on an account.

- *Office Test*: The Office Test registry key is a common target for attackers because that registry allows you to set a random **Dynamic Link Library** (**DLL**), or code that can be used by multiple programs at the same time, to execute every single time an Office application is started.

- *Office Forms*: These are templates used in various Office applications and can be compromised via a malicious form being uploaded and automatically loaded when an Office application is started.

- *Outlook Home Page*: This is a legacy feature within Office, which means that it is backward-compatible with older versions of Office. It allows a user to customize the appearance of a folder and can be compromised through code injection and remote code execution, which could execute when the compromised folder is clicked on.

- *Outlook Rules*: These are conditions put on your Outlook inbox that can set up filtering, forwarding, and automatic replies. An attack would compromise these by creating a malicious Outlook rule that would be executed when the attack sent a specific email to execute the rule.

- *Add-Ins*: These include the ability to add features to your individual Office programs, such as Word or Excel. These can be compromised by an attacker injecting code into a few different libraries, then remotely executing the code and maintaining persistence on the account.

The sub-techniques show a variety of ways that Office 365 can be abused by malicious users, especially because it is a common target. One of the procedural examples of the technique is APT32, an APT group based out of Vietnam, replacing Microsoft Outlook's **VbaProfect.OTM** (**VBA** is **Visual Basic for Applications**) file to install a backdoor macro to maintain persistence on someone's account.

Steps for mitigation are to enable the Attack Surface Reduction rules on Windows 10 machines, to disable Office VBA macros from executing, and to always update your software, among other steps. For detection, it is recommended that you implement monitoring on your application logs, specifically for third parties that leverage Microsoft Office, and monitor for newly constructed files that may leverage the application startup features.

Typically, when you use Office 365, you also use Azure **Active Directory** (**AD**) for account and account permissions management. Active Directory is a database that connects users with respective resources or permissions that are needed to get their work completed. AD is one form of account management, and there are over one billion users of Azure AD currently, which makes it an obvious target for monitoring as part of your security best practices. The Azure AD matrix comprises the following tactics and techniques:

- Initial Access

  - Valid Accounts

- Persistence

  - Account Manipulation, Create Account, and Valid Accounts

- Privilege Escalation

  - Domain Policy Modification and Valid Account

- Defense Evasion

  - Domain Policy Modification and Valid Account

- Credential Access

  - Brute Force, Forge Web Credentials, Multi-Factor Authentication Request Generation, Steal Application Access Token, and Unsecured Credentials

- Discovery

  - Account Discovery, Cloud Service Dashboard, Cloud Service Discovery, Permission Groups Discovery, and Software Discovery

- Impact

  - Endpoint Denial of Service and Network Denial of Service

Similar to Office 365, it is a rather small matrix compared to the generic cloud one and others, and from looking at the matrix, you see some similar techniques such as Valid Accounts and Account Manipulation. One interesting note is that while there are similar techniques, there are different sub-techniques listed; for example, Account Manipulation in the Office 365 matrix has two sub-techniques, whereas Account Manipulation has three sub-techniques in the Azure AD matrix. One technique that we'll take a closer look at in this matrix is Endpoint Denial of Service in the Impact tactic, which has three sub-techniques:

- *Service Exhaustion Flood*: This is when a software vulnerability in the service is exploited to the point that it causes the service to crash and become unusable for other users

- *Application Exhaustion Flood*: This is when a software vulnerability in the application is exploited to the point that it causes the application to crash and become unusable for other users

- *Application or System Exploitation*: This is when a software vulnerability in the application or system is exploited to the point that it causes the application or system to crash and become unusable for other users

Endpoint DoS at its core is any time that a service, system, or application is exploited to the point that it is no longer responsive and crashes, causing an outage for other users. Common examples of this are HTTP floods, SYN floods, and **Distributed Denial of Service** (**DDoS**) attacks. DoS and DDoS attacks are very common because they can be easily executed, and one procedural example is of the **Sandworm Team**, a Russian threat group that was able to execute an attack against the government of the country of Georgia and cause an outage in 2019. There are also multiple open source tools and scripts that can be used to execute DoS and DDoS attacks. Some mitigation steps are through implementing firewall rules for rate-limiting, implementing load-balancing where possible, and leveraging features from **Content Delivery Networks** (**CDNs**) that specialize in DoS and DDoS mitigation. For detection, you can analyze traffic patterns, looking specifically for large numbers of denials, or from a specific header, and in general analyzing data for unusual or unexpected spikes.

A non-Microsoft product, and one that is gaining traction as an option for replacing traditional endpoints, is Google Workspaces. Google Workspaces currently has over three billion users and is continuing to grow. The matrix for Google Workspace looks like the following:

- Initial Access

  - Phishing and Valid Accounts

- Persistence

  - Account Manipulation, Create Account, and Valid Accounts

- Privilege Escalation

  - Valid Accounts

- Defense Evasion

  - Use Alternate Authentication Material and Valid Accounts

- Credential Access

  - Brute Force, Forge Web Credentials, Multi-Factor Authentication Request Generation, Steal Application Access Token, Steal Web Session Cookie, and Unsecured Credentials

- Discovery

  - Account Discovery, Cloud Service Dashboard, Cloud Service Discovery, Permission Groups Discovery, and Software Discovery

- Lateral Movement

  - Internal Spearphishing and Use Alternate Authentication Material

- Collection

  - Data from Information Repositories and Email Collection

- Impact

  - Endpoint Denial of Service and Network Denial of Service

This is obviously a larger matrix than both Office 365 and Azure AD, but that's because Google Workspaces works like a virtual endpoint and carries out more functions than Office 365 and Azure AD. One of the techniques worth digging into is Use Alternative Authentication Material in the Defense Evasion tactic, which has two sub-techniques:

- *Application Access Token*: This is a form of MFA that makes an API call on behalf of the user to authenticate. Common Application Access Tokens are used via Duo and Microsoft Authenticator.

- *Web Session Cookie*: These are server-side files that contain user data, which could be anything from authentication to browsing data, and are cleared when a user's session is over, such as logging out or exiting a program.

MFA in general is extremely common, and if it's not implemented in your environment, we strongly suggest that you set it up. With MFA, physical tokens such as RSA Tokens or YubiKeys, or software tokens from apps such as Authenticator and Duo, are used for something you have a requirement for.

Attackers will try to compromise MFA by sending multiple pushes for a compromised password in the hope that an end user accepts it. The attacker will then have access to the account and might be able to move laterally within the organization to carry out their actions on objectives. There have been multiple cases in which MFA has been hijacked, one example of which was undertaken by APT29, a Russian APT group that commonly compromises SAML (a form of web authentication) tokens. Another case is the Uber compromise of 2022, which started from an attacker spamming an end user with authentication pushes that the end user eventually accepted, and then the attacker was able to execute scripts to escalate their privilege and complete a full compromise of Uber. Some steps that can be taken for mitigation are to limit credential overlaps across systems, which means requiring users to have potentially multiple sets of credentials to mitigate lateral movement and implement the **principle of least privilege**; this means only giving users the level of access that they absolutely need to conduct their job and typically means limiting who has admin privileges.

Other forms of cloud services are SaaS and IaaS. SaaS is when applications are cloud-based and it is becoming more and more common for application offerings to provide SaaS versions. The SaaS model looks like this:

- Initial Access
    - Drive-by Compromise, Phishing, Trusted Relationship, and Valid Accounts

- Persistence
    - Account Manipulation and Valid Account

- Privilege Escalation
    - Valid Account

- Defense Evasion
    - Use Alternate Authentication Material and Valid Accounts

- Credential Access
    - Brute Force, Forge Web Credentials, Multi-Factor Authentication Request Generation, Steal Application Access Token, Steal Web Session Cookie, and Unsecured Credentials

- Discovery
    - Account Discovery, Cloud Service Discovery, Permission Groups Discovery, and Software Discovery

- Lateral Movement
    - Internal Spearphishing, Taint Shared Content, and Use Alternate Authentication Material

- Collection
    - Automated Collection and Data from Information Repositories

- Impact
    - Account Access Removal, Endpoint Denial of Service, and Network Denial of Service

The SaaS model usually provides flexibility in the scalability of an application, in uptime, and ideally lower overhead with the management of the SaaS applications. Out of this matrix, we'll take a deeper look at the Data from Information Repositories technique from the Collection tactic, which has two sub-techniques:

- *Confluence*: This is a collaboration space bought by Atlassian, used for information sharing and creating team spaces, and it is typically a central repository for creating organizational processes and storing information.

- *Code Repositories*: These are archives of the code that is actively being worked on. A notable code repository tool is GitHub, where developers have the ability to pull down code, submit new code, and run code to test it.

Information repositories are commonly targeted by attackers that are looking to exfiltrate data, looking for credentials that might be shared within the information repositories, or looking for other pertinent information such as client lists or system data. It's very common to see teams share company-sensitive data on Confluence pages or for passwords or keys to be hardcoded into the code in the repositories. There are a number of attackers that have targeted information repositories as part of their attacks, but some of the notable ones are APT 28, a Russian APT group, and FoxKitten, a hacker group attributed to Iran. Some steps that can be taken to mitigate security risks within information repositories is to establish a set of secure coding practices, so developers do not hardcode any passwords or keys into their code. Another step is to audit all code repositories and information repositories to review shared confidential information. A different way to monitor and detect these actions is to review application logs and review and third-party access to the information content. Another step would be to implement monitoring on login sessions and what pages users attempt to access, especially in cases where they might not have permission to do so.

There is also the growing popularity of IaaS. IaaS is a form of cloud computing that offers computing power, networking resources, and storage on demand and is growing in popularity due to the ease of setting up failover sites and the ease of scalability. Common examples of IaaS are VirtualBox, AWS, Azure, and DigitalOcean. The IaaS matrix looks like the following:

- Initial Access

  - Exploit Public Facing Application, Trusted Relationship, and Valid Accounts

- Execution

  - User Execution

- Persistence

  - Account Manipulation, Create Account, Implant Internal Image, and Valid Accounts

- Privilege Escalation

  - Valid Accounts

- Defense Evasion

  - Impair Defenses, Modify Cloud Compute Infrastructure, Unused/Unsupported Cloud Regions, Use Alternate Authentication Material, and Valid Accounts

- Credential Access

  - Brute Force, Forge Web Credentials, Multi-Factor Authentication Request Generation, Network Sniffing, and Unsecured Credentials

- Discovery

  - Account Discovery, Cloud Infrastructure Discovery, Cloud Service Dashboard, Cloud Service Discovery, Cloud Storage Object Discovery, Network Service Discovery, Network Sniffing, Password Policy Discovery, Permission Groups Discovery, Software Discovery, System Information Discovery, System Location Discovery, and System Network Connections Discovery

- Lateral Movement

  - Use Alternate Authentication Material

- Collection

  - Automated Collection, Data from Cloud Storage Object, Data from Information Repositories, and Data Staged

- Exfiltration

  - Transfer Data to Cloud Account

- Impact

  - Data Destruction, Data Encrypted for Impact, Defacement, Endpoint Denial of Service, Network Denial of Service, and Resource Hijacking

As you can see here, it is the largest of the specialized cloud matrices. One technique that we'll take a closer look at is Modify Cloud Compute Infrastructure in the Defense Evasion tactic, which has four sub-techniques:

- *Create Snapshot*: **Snapshots** are point-in-time copies of data. They are used heavily in disaster recovery planning and backups in general. An attacker might create a snapshot to bypass restrictions or to add new rules, such as making network changes to allow SSH traffic.

- *Create Cloud Instance*: These are virtual server instances, and an attacker might create a cloud instance to bypass firewall rules or permissions.

- *Delete Cloud Instance*: This is where a virtual server is removed. An attacker might delete a cloud instance in an effort to cover their tracks by removing forensic information.

- *Revert Cloud Instance*: This is to go back to an earlier state in that instance. An attacker might want to do this to help evade detection after conducting malicious actions or to remove evidence.

This technique was chosen because it only appears in the IaaS and overarching cloud boards, as it is different from any other cloud matrix. An attacker might modify cloud compute infrastructure in the form of adding or removing virtual servers or instances, enabling or disabling services, and so on. These actions are typically conducted in an attempt to bypass permission or other restrictions or used as a pivot point because once a malicious action is conducted, an attacker can easily remove the instance, which helps cover up their tracks. The thing with IaaS is that as cloud infrastructure becomes more popular, which is clearly happening rapidly, these types of attacks will continue to occur and occur more frequently; therefore, there have been a large number of APT groups that have used cloud infrastructure in their compromises. For mitigation, this is actually one of the harder techniques to mitigate because it's based on the abuse of a normal action. The main steps that you can take are to ensure that proper privileges are in place to restrict who can stand up and spin down cloud resources and restrict any pages that have confidential data, and these steps in and of themselves can be laborious and sometimes detrimental to fast-moving teams, so this is a case where you want to rely more on detection. Some detection steps can be to establish logging for starting, stopping, and modifying instances. For example, in our organization, we have alerts that are configured to be triggered when an instance is spun up with overly permissive permissions so that we can investigate this, and even though it's typically done so as an oversight, it's good to have that "trust but verify" mindset.

As you can see, we have now taken a deeper look at all of the cloud-related matrices that are currently available for the MITRE ATT&CK Framework. There are differences in each matrix, and this is a great instance of having to choose the correct one and the applicable techniques and sub-techniques to monitor and cover in your environment. It's also important to understand what you should monitor for detection and mitigation as more and more environments transition to either hybrid or full cloud environments. In the next section, we'll cover the Windows framework matrix.

A deep dive into the techniques in the Windows framework

Windows machines make up over 200 million enterprise users with many high-target organizations being primarily Windows users, such as the US government. Due to the number of Windows users, roughly 80% of all malware attacks target Windows users specifically. That means that you have to be extra vigilant if you work on a security team in a Windows environment and need to ensure that proper logging, detections, risk categorizations, and detections are put in place. The Windows matrix encompasses all controls and is not broken down based on the Operating System (OS) version or if it is a server or endpoint, so there is definitely a level of tweaking that is necessary when reviewing the matrix. The matrix in its entirety looks like the following:

- Initial Access

  Drive-by Compromise, Exploit Public Facing Application, External Remote Services, Hardware Additions, Phishing, Replication Through Removable Media, Supply Chain Compromise, Trusted Relationship, and Valid Accounts

- Execution

  Command and Scripting Interpreter, Exploitation for Client Execution, Inter-Process Communication, Native API, Scheduled Task/Job, Shared Modules, Software Deployment Tools, System Services, User Execution, and Windows Management Instrumentation

- Persistence

  Account Manipulation, BITS Jobs, Boot or Logon Autostart Execution, Boot or Logon Initialization Scripts, Browser Extensions, Compromise Client Software Binary, Create Account, Create or Modify System Process, Event Triggered Execution, External Remote Services, Hijack Execution Flow, Modify Authentication Process, Office Application Startup, Pre-OS Boot, Scheduled Task/Job, Server Software Component, Traffic Signaling, and Valid Accounts

- Privilege Escalation

  Abuse Elevation Control Mechanism, Access Token Manipulation, Boot or Logon Autostart Execution, Boot or Logon Initialization Scripts, Create or Modify Process, Domain Policy Modification, Escape to Host, Event Triggered Execution, Exploitation for Privilege Escalation, Hijack Execution Flow, Process Injection, Scheduled Task/Job, and Valid Accounts

- Defense Evasion

  Abuse Elevation Control Mechanism, Access Token Manipulation, BITS Jobs, Debugger Evasion, Deobfuscate/Decode Files or Information, Direct Volume Access, Domain Policy Modification, Execution Guardrails, Exploitation for Defense Evasion, Files and Directory Permissions Modification, Hide Artifacts, Hijack Execution Flow, Impair Defense, Indicator Removal, Indirect Command Execution, Masquerading, Modify Authentication Process, Modify Registry, Obfuscated Files or Information, Pre-OS Boot, Process Injection, Reflective Code Loading, Rogue Domain Controller, Rootkit, Subvert Trust Controls, System Binary Proxy Execution, System Script Proxy Execution, Template Injection, Traffic Signaling, Trusted Developer Utilities Proxy Execution, Use Alternate Authentication Material, Valid Accounts, Virtualization/Sandbox Evasion, and XSL Script Processing

- Credential Access

  Adversary-in-the-Middle, Brute Force, Credentials from Password Stores, Exploitation for Credential Access, Forced Authentication, Forge Web Credentials, Input Capture, Modify Authentication Process, Multi-Factor Authentication Interception, Multi Factor Authentication Request Generation, Network Sniffing, OS Credential Dumping, Steal or Forge Kerberos Tickets, Steal Web Session Cookie, and Unsecured Credentials

- Discovery

  Account Discovery, Application Window Discovery, Browser Bookmark Discovery, Debugger Evasion, Domain Trust Discovery, File and Directory Discovery, Group Policy Discovery, Network Service Discovery, Network Share Discovery, Network Sniffing, Password Policy Discovery, Peripheral Device Discovery, Permission Groups Discovery, Process Discovery, Query Registry, Remote System Discovery, Software Discovery, System Information Discovery, System Location Discovery, System Network Configuration Discovery, System Network Connections Discovery, System Owner/User Discovery, System Service Discovery, System Time Discovery, and Virtualization/Sandbox Evasion

- Lateral Movement

  Exploitation of Remote Services, Internal Spearphishing, Lateral Tool Transfer, Remote Service Session Hijacking, Remote Services, Replication Through Removable Media, Software Deployment Tools, Taint Shared Content, and Use Alternate Authentication Material

- Collection

  Adversary-in-the-Middle, Archive Collected Data, Audio Capture, Automated Collection, Browser Session Hijacking, Clipboard Data, Data from Information Repositories, Data from Local System, Data from Network Shared Drive, Data from Removable Media, Data Staged, Email Collection, Input Capture, Screen Capture, and Video Capture

- Command and Control

  Application Layer Protocol, Communication Through Removable Media, Data Encoding, Data Obfuscation, Dynamic Resolution, Encrypted Channel, Fallback Channels, Ingress Tool Transfer, Multi-Stage Channels, Non-Application Layer Protocol, Non-Standard Port, Protocol Tunneling, Proxy, Remote Access Software, Traffic Signaling, and Web Service

- Exfiltration

  Automated Exfiltration, Data Transfer Size Limits, Exfiltration Over Alternative Protocol, Exfiltration Over C2 Channel, Exfiltration Over Other Network Medium, Exfiltration Over Physical Medium, Exfiltration Over Web Service, and Scheduled Transfer

- Impact

    Account Access Removal, Data Destruction, Data Encrypted for Impact, Data Manipulation, Defacement, Disk Wipe, Endpoint Denial of Service, Firmware Corruption, Inhibit System Recovery, Network Denial of Service, Resource Hijacking, and Service Stop System Shutdown/ Reboot

As you can see, there are significantly more techniques than the cloud matrices had and that is due to a few different factors. The first is that as mentioned earlier, Windows systems are high-target areas and have been around longer than cloud infrastructure. So, when 80% of malware attacks are focused on Windows systems, there are naturally going to be more techniques. The second reason is as we mentioned, it encompasses Windows servers and Windows endpoints instead of breaking them down. Finally, the third reason is due to how the Windows infrastructure is set up with various locations for logs such as Windows Events logs, Application logs, and Security logs. Due to the fact that there is only one Windows matrix, we'll dig into a few different techniques. The first one is Supply Chain Compromise in the Initial Access tactic. We chose this one because while there are some mitigation steps that can be taken, it is largely out of your control because it's based on vendors and third-party infrastructure. The technique has three sub-techniques, which are the following:

- *Compromise Software Dependencies and Development Tools*: This is when third-party libraries and other code dependencies or the tools, such as compilers, are compromised. An attack would compromise that dependency and then that compromises the data for any code that relies on that dependency.

- *Compromise Software Supply Chain*: This is when software is compromised prior to delivering it to the end user, which could lead to data or system-level compromises.

- *Compromise Hardware Supply Chain*: This is when physical devices are compromised during production from a third-party provider, which could compromise boot startup actions, and so on.

Not only is this technique largely out of your control for some of the mitigation because it relies on a third party's security practices but it is also the technique used for the famous SolarWinds compromise, which affected 18,000 customers due to the APT group APT29 from Russia being able to hijack an update and create a Trojan. This then allowed network-level access on any customer that ran the update. A Trojan is a type of malware that is disguised as a legitimate file and refers to the Trojan Horse used by the ancient Greeks. While the SolarWinds compromise is the most notable recent supply chain compromise, there have been a number of APT groups that have used this strategy to compromise corporations, because if successful, they have the ability to impact a large number of customers. For mitigation, because it's reliant on the third party, you can implement vulnerability scanning and perform software updates when they are available, but of course, as the SolarWinds compromise showed, that's not always the case. Another step that can be taken is scanning for vulnerabilities in any code dependencies, so expanding from traditional vulnerability scanning, and implementing a security vetting process for any third-party vulnerabilities to complete your due diligence. For detection, you should implement a hash-checking process to ensure any hashes of updates match the provided hashes to ensure that the file has not been altered in any way.

The next control is Remote Services under the Lateral Movement technique. This was chosen because on Windows systems, not only can one use putty and SSH to/from systems but there is also **Remote Desktop Protocol (RDP)** natively, so there are additional options for remotely connecting to and from a system. There are five sub-techniques in Remote Services, which are the following:

- *Remote Desktop Protocol*: RDP is a protocol that comes as a standard on Windows systems and it allows a valid user to log in remotely to/from their computer. If an attacker compromises a valid user account, they can then utilize RDP to connect to various hosts within the network.

- *SMB/Windows Admin Shares*: SMB is a protocol used for sharing printers across a network. An attacker would compromise this to be able to access file shares to compromise data.

- *Distributed Component Object Model*: **Distributed Component Object Model (DCOM)** allows for sharing of software and executable code. An attacker might compromise a legitimate account to use DCOM to carry out actions on objectives.

- *Virtual Network Computing*: **Virtual Network Computing (VNC)** is specific to screen-sharing rather than true remote connection and uses system credentials. An attacker would want to use VNC for the authentication piece and to compromise data by opening files once they are authenticated.

- *Windows Remote Management*: **Windows Remote Management (WinRM)** is a protocol and service that allows an authenticated user to remotely execute commands, and the attacker would want to compromise a legitimate account to leverage the WinRM service.

Remote services in general are a common area for attackers to hijack and then perform actions as a legitimate logged-in user. Some attackers will use what are known as **Remote Access Trojans (RATs)**, which are a type of malware to help carry out actions, and this is where an attacker would compromise a legitimate user using a RAT and have remote access ability to list out directory contents, traverse the network, and so on. Some mitigation steps that would be helpful are ensuring MFA is used even in cases where there is remote authentication and ensuring the **principle of least privilege** is applied to all user accounts. For detection, there are a few steps that you can take, assuming that you have inclusive logs. The first would be to alert on logs where the login location and MFA acceptance are different locations or locations not associated with a given enterprise, that is, Europe, China, Australia, and India, for example, or set up logging for authentications via remote access, but that could be noisy depending on how many people are in your organization. If anything, we would set up an alert for a large amount of data exports or resources used or connections to multiple machines remotely.

The next technique we are going to look at is the Input Capture technique in the Credential Access tactic, which has the following four sub-techniques:

- *Keylogging*: This is a method using either software, API calls, or registry drivers to read every key that is typed in a way to compromise data and credentials

- *Graphical User Interface Input Capture*: **Graphical User Interface (GUI)** Input Capture is typically a popup or malicious program that appears to be legitimate and prompts the end user for information to capture said information, such as credentials to leverage for future attacks

- *Web Portal Capture*: This is typically where code is injected into a web portal login page, which then captures any keystrokes of clicks that the end user executes

- *Credential API Hooking*: This is where code is injected to hijack the Windows API calls in order to execute remote code or redirect code

Input capture is a tactic that has been used by many attackers; some notable ones are APT39, an Iranian APT group that captured mouse movement and clicks, and the Chinese-backed APT3, which has used keyloggers to capture keystrokes in encrypted files. In the case of these techniques, specific mitigation steps can be tough; some steps can be taken, such as running regular vulnerability scanning, educating end users on the security best practices, and restricting permissions—essentially to have a mature security posture for the organization. For detection steps, organizations can implement monitoring on file modifications, implement monitoring on file creation, and implement monitoring on Windows registry keys and API executions. The last technique in the Windows matrix that we'll review is the Adversary-in-the-Middle technique in the Collection tactic, which has the following three sub-techniques:

- *LLMNR/NBT-NS Poisoning and SMB Relay*: **Link-Local Multicast Name Resolution (LLMNR)/ NetBIOS Name Service (NBT-NS)** are protocols that are used for host identification. An attacker would inject incorrect host data in an attempt to redirect traffic and complete data compromise.

- *ARP Cache Poisoning*: **Address Resolution Protocol (ARP)** is the protocol responsible for connecting IP addresses to physical machines. Attackers will input false information into the ARP cache, which then re-routes IPs so the information flows from the physical device to the attacker to the internet.

- *DHCP Spoofing*: **Dynamic Host Configuration Protocol (DHCP)** is the protocol that manages all of the IPs that are allocated to a network. DHCP spoofing is when an attacker responds to a DHCP request so that traffic flows through them first, compromising any data in that traffic.

Man-in-the-middle attacks are fairly common and can be conducted over the sub-techniques listed previously or others, such as intercepting network traffic on an unencrypted network. Some of the more notorious man-in-the-middle attacks were that of the Lazarus Group, a North Korean hacker group, which collected credentials and was responsible for the hack on Sony in 2014. There are multiple tools that can be used for man-in-the-middle attacks such as Empire, Pupy, and Cleaver. Some steps for mitigation would be to implement encryption on any communications, disable any legacy protocols or protocols that wouldn't be used in your network, and user security awareness training for following the best security practices.

As you can see from the techniques that we looked into and at the matrix alone, there are a lot of security considerations when working in a Windows environment due to it being a high target. If you work in a Windows environment, you'll want to remain diligent and constantly review your risk and controls to see whether you can build out detection and mitigation. Next, we'll review the macOS framework as it is the second largest type of endpoint for enterprise clients.

A deep dive into the techniques in the macOS framework

While there is a significantly higher number of Windows users than macOS users, there are still over 100 million macOS users and macOS endpoints are growing in popularity, especially in the private business sector and specifically for tech companies. Overall, the difference in size means that there are fewer attacks that are targeted at macOS endpoints, but that certainly doesn't mean that there are none. Additionally, it's important to note that there are a significant number of techniques and sub-techniques that are different between the macOS and Windows matrices due to how the base OS works and how the filesystems are set up. If anything, macOS aligns more closely with the Linux OS. Similarly to the Windows section, we'll dig into a few different techniques and sub-techniques:

- Initial Access

  - Drive-by Compromise, Exploit Public Facing Application, External Remote Services, Hardware Additions, Phishing, Supply Chain Compromise, Trusted Relationship, and Valid Accounts

- Execution

  - Command and Scripting Interpreter, Exploitation for Client Execution, Inter-Process Communications, Native API, Scheduled Task/Job, Software Deployment Tools, System Services, and User Execution

- Persistence

  - Account Manipulation, Boot or Logon Autostart Execution, Boot or Logon Initialization Scripts, Browser Extensions, Compromise Client Software Binary, Create Account, Create or Modify System Process, Event Triggered Execution, External Remote Services, Hijack Execution Flow, Modify Authentication Process, Pre-OS Boot, Scheduled Task/Job, Server Software Component, Traffic Signaling, and Valid Accounts

- Privilege Escalation

  - Abuse Elevation Control Mechanism, Boot or Logon Autostart Execution, Boot or Logon Initialization Scripts, Create or Modify System Process, Event Triggered Execution, Exploitation for Privilege Escalation, Hijack Execution Flow, Process Injection, Scheduled Task/Job, and Valid Accounts

- Defense Evasion

  - Abuse Elevation Control Mechanism, Debugger Evasion, Deobfuscate/Decode Files or Information, Execution Guardrails, Exploitation for Defense Evasion, File and Directory Permissions Modification, Hide Artifacts, Hijack Execution Flow, Impair Defenses, Indicator Removal on Host, Masquerading, Modify Authentication Process, Obfuscated Files or Information, Plist File Modification, Pre-OS Boot, Process Injection, Reflective Code Loading, Rootkit, Subvert Trust Controls, System Binary Proxy Execution, Traffic Signaling, Valid Accounts, and Virtualization/Sandbox Evasion

- Credential Access

  - Adversary-in-the-Middle, Brute Force, Credentials from Password Stores, Exploitation for Credential Access, Forge Web Credentials, Input Capture, Modify Authentication Process, Multi Factor Authentication Interception, Multi Factor Authentication Request Generation, Network Sniffing, OS Credential Dumping, Steal or Forge Kerberos Tickets, Steal Web Session Cookie, and Unsecured Credentials

- Discovery

  - Account Discovery, Application Window Discovery, Browser Bookmark Discovery, Debugger Evasion, File and Directory Discovery, Network Service Discovery, Network Sniffing, Password Policy Discovery, Permission Groups Discovery, Process Discovery, Remote System Discovery, Software Discovery, System Information Discovery, System Location Discovery, System Network Configuration Discovery, System Network Connections Discovery, System Owner/User Discovery, System Service Discovery, and Virtualization/Sandbox Evasion

- Lateral Movement

  - Exploitation of Remote Services, Internal Spearphishing, Lateral Tool Transfer, Remote Service Session Hijacking, Remote Services, Software Deployment Tools, and Taint Shared Content

- Collection

  - Adversary-in-the-Middle, Archive Collected Data, Audio Capture, Automated Collection, Clipboard Data, Data from Information Repositories, Data from Local System, Data from Network Shared Drive, Data from Removable Media, Data Staged, Email Collection, Input Capture, Screen Capture, and Video Capture

- Command and Control

  - Application Layer Protocol, Communication Through Removable Media, Data Encoding, Data Obfuscation, Dynamic Resolution, Encrypted Channel, Fallback Channels, Ingress Tool Transfer, Multi-Stage Channels, Non-Application Layer Protocol, Non-Standard Port, Protocol Tunneling, Proxy, Remote Access Software, Traffic Signaling, and Web Service.

- Exfiltration

  - Automated Exfiltration, Data Transfer Size Limits, Exfiltration Over Alternative Protocol, Exfiltration Over C2 Channel, Exfiltration Over Other Network Medium, Exfiltration Over Other Network Medium, Exfiltration Over Physical Medium, Exfiltration Over Web Service, and Scheduled Transfer

- Impact

  - Account Access Removal, Data Destruction, Data Encrypted for Impact, Data Manipulation, Defacement, Disk Wipe, Endpoint Denial of Service, Firmware Corruption, Inhibit System Recovery, Network Denial of Service, Resource Hijacking, Service Stop, and System Shutdown/Reboot

The first technique that will be analyzed is Masquerading in the Defense Evasion tactic, which has the following sub-techniques:

- *Invalid Code Signature*: This is when an attacker attempts to input an incorrect signature and pass it as a valid code signature to get a false level of authenticity

- *Right-to-Left Override*: This is the action of using the **Right-to-Left Override** (RTLO) characters, a special character in Unicode, to disguise a string or text to make it appear legitimate and unthreatening

- *Rename System Utilities*: This is the action of renaming any system utilities in an attempt to evade detection and bypass security measures

- *Masquerade Task or Service*: This is the action of renaming any automated tasks or services in an attempt to evade detection, bypass security measures, and make the tasks appear benign

- *Match Legitimate Name or Location*: This is the action of changing the name or location of a file or resource in an attempt to evade detection, bypass security measures, and make the updated filename and location appear benign

- *Space after Filename*: This is the action of adding a literal space after the name of the file, resource, utility, task, or service to make the name appear as a different one than the legitimate name without standing out in an attempt to evade detection, bypass security measures, and make the file name with a space appear benign

Masquerading by definition is the act of showing a false pretense and pretending that something is other than it is, which occurs with websites, files, and so on. There are multiple different types of attacks that can be attributed to masquerading, primarily those associated with phishing, where malicious links will try to look as if they are legitimate to have a higher rate of clicks. There have been numerous attacks and APT groups that have relied on masquerading as part of their attack pattern, such as the Russian group APT28 and the Vietnam-based group APT32, to name a few, and these show that masquerading is a prevalent threat that all organizations should consider and attempt to mitigate and detect. Some steps for mitigation would be to require code signatures, which would ensure that any code added was legitimate, and another mitigation step to take would be to restrict file and directory permissions. Steps for detection would be to implement alerting for file hash changes, alerts for file metadata that includes RTLO characters, and alerts for command execution.

The next technique is Hide Artifacts, also in the Defense Evasion tactic, which has eight sub-techniques:

- *Hidden Files and Directories*: Files and directories have the ability to be marked as hidden; however, that means that without explicitly unhiding files or commands on the command line, an attack can go unnoticed.

- *Hidden Users*: Attackers will occasionally create new users and hide the user profiles to evade detection. This can be done on Windows, Linux, and macOS.

- *Hidden Window*: This is when an attacker hides a normal application window on macOS by changing one of the flags on the property list files. This means that an attacker can run a program while the user does not see it.

- *Hidden File System*: This is when an attacker hides a file share or multiple directories. This could be done to have hidden malicious files to execute or to hide their own tools.

- *Run Virtual Instance*: This is where an attacker might run a virtual machine in order to create a shared filesystem and delete their trail after files are transferred to the host systems.

- *VBA Stomping*: This is when an attacker injects malicious code into a VB application or library.

- *Email Hiding Rules*: Email rules are used for setting filters and creating folders; however, an attacker would want to create rules to modify emails and/or delete emails to evade detection.

- *Resource Forking*: A **resource fork** is a section of a file in macOS. Attackers would want to inject code into the resource forks to hide the code and then remotely execute it.

The point of hiding artifacts is to ideally evade detection in any form, and as you can see, there are multiple ways to accomplish this. In fact, there are multiple tools and types of malware such as Keydnap, InvisiMole, and Altomac that can automatically help you hide artifacts for both legitimate and nefarious purposes. There have also been a large number of hacking groups, such as the Lazarus Group, APT 28, and APT 32, to name a few, that have used hidden artifacts as part of their compromises. Implementing mitigation can be complicated with hidden artifacts due to the fact that this is primarily abusing how a feature is supposed to work, but there are a few steps that can be taken. The first is if your endpoints are joined on a domain, you should be able to enforce a policy that restricts hidden users from being created. The second is to implement application controls in the form of not allowing unapproved virtualization software to be downloaded. Then, the last step is to enforce monitoring of audit logs, especially when it comes to email. For detection, you will rely on the monitoring that has been put in place to look for deletion email rules, to review the PLIST files on macOS to ensure no changes have been made to the **Hide500Users** setting, and to set up alerts for remote code and command execution.

The third technique that we'll take a look at is the Proxy technique under the Command and Control tactic. Proxies in general can be a perfectly legitimate part of your network setup, but there are ways that attackers can leverage proxies to their advantage. A proxy server essentially acts as a gateway between the end users and the internet and has the ability to provide some security checks and balances through what traffic is permitted. There are four sub-techniques for proxy:

- *Internal Proxy*: This proxy sits inside the organizational network and has the ability to restrict sites and content that is not work-related. An attack might leverage an internal proxy to restrict the number of outbound network calls made to their command-and-control server, which helps them evade detection.

- *External Proxy*: This is primarily used by an attacker because it can mask their destination IP for their command-and-control traffic and redirect traffic from specific ports. It is also known as a **reverse proxy**.

- *Multi-Hop Proxy*: This is the process of combining multiple proxies to mask the location of traffic, which makes it much harder to detect malicious action and mitigate it.

- *Domain Fronting*: This is the process of using multiple different domain names in the various layers of a web connection, which helps an attacker evade detection from monitoring while they quietly connect to a target.

As mentioned, proxy servers and systems are completely legitimate and used regularly in networks, which makes them valuable tools for attackers to leverage. Common proxies that you'll see attackers leverage are Tor nodes, which are access points that work like proxies, but even with Tor nodes, there are perfectly legitimate uses as well. Some remote-access trojans and other malware even have the ability to work or set up reverse proxies to help evade detection, such as the Cardinal RAT. Some steps that can be taken for mitigation are to implement restrictive access control lists for both inbound and outbound traffic, filter and monitor network traffic, and implement SSL/TLS inspection. Some steps that can be taken for detection are primarily focused on creating alerts based on the filtered network traffic that is being monitored.

The final technique for macOS that we'll look into is the Defacement technique under the Impact tactic. **Defacement** by definition is the process or action of spoiling the surface or the appearance of something and it is a technique that is very common with website defacement. There are two sub-techniques:

- *Internal Defacement*: This is the action of changing the appearance of internal systems and is seen with most ransomware attacks where the screen will show that the files are encrypted, and a ransom must be paid to get the decryption key

- *External Defacement*: This is typically the action of changing the appearance of a website and can be done for hacktivism, to damage the reputation of the company or organization, or for bragging rights

Defacement techniques are common, especially external defacement for websites that are based on WordPress or other web frameworks such as Joomla. The reason for that is because of the open source nature of some of the web frameworks; specifically for WordPress, a leading contributor is the number of plugins. One of the more notable defacements was in 2020 when 51 different US government websites were defaced by Iranian hackers, or when the Ashley Madison website was compromised in 2015 by the hacktivist group known as the Impact Team, who eventually leaked 60 GB of data. Steps for mitigation are primarily focused on ensuring all software and software packages are up to date, and ensuring all data is backed up so that in the case of a defacement you can easily restore any systems to working order. For detection, there is the obvious option of seeing that a system has been defaced, but other steps include monitoring web and application logs, and monitoring file creation and modification.

Even though macOS is not impacted by the majority of cyber attacks, it can still be compromised and impacted. A great example is that there were two different zero-day vulnerabilities for macOS that were released in quarter 1 of 2022 alone. The first zero-day was *CVE-2022-32893*, which was a vulnerability in WebKit, Apple's HTML rendering software, that allowed running unauthorized code. The second was *CVE-2022-32894*, which allowed an application to execute arbitrary code with kernel-level privileges. That alone shows that macOS is still being targeted in general, which is why we need to analyze the macOS matrix and apply mitigation and risk evaluation where applicable. In the next section, we'll take a look at the network matrix and dig into a few different techniques.

A deep dive into the techniques in the network framework

Now that endpoints have been covered, we'll take a deeper look at the network matrix. One interesting note about this matrix is that network is very vague, as there can be many different components that make up a network, and that means that the implementation of the mitigation and detection strategies will have to be heavily tweaked to fit your environment. There is only one matrix, whereas we saw in the cloud, there were multiple, so that means that there are some controls that won't apply to your environment at all, depending on how it is configured. The network matrix looks like this:

- Initial Access
  - Exploit Public Facing Application

- Execution
  - Command and Scripting Interpreter

- Persistence
  - Modify Authentication Process, Pre-OS Boot, and Traffic Signaling

- Defense Evasion
  - Impair Defenses, Indicator Removal on Host, Modify Authentication Process, Modify System Image, Network Boundary Bridging, Pre-OS Boot, Traffic Signaling, and Weaken Encryption

- Credential Access
  - Brute Force, Input Capture, Modify Authentication Process, and Network Sniffing

- Discovery
  - File and Directory Discovery, Network Service Discovery, Network Sniffing, Password Policy Discovery, Remote System Discovery, System Information Discovery, System Network Configuration Discovery, and System Network Connections Discovery

- Collection
  - Data from Configuration Repository, Data from Local System, and Input Capture

- Command and Control
  - Non-Application Layer Protocol, Proxy, and Traffic Signaling

- Exfiltration
  - Automated Exfiltration

- Impact
  - Firmware Corruption and System Shutdown/Reboot

After looking at the matrix, you can also see that it is significantly smaller than the Windows and macOS matrices. The first technique we'll examine is the Exploit Public Facing Applications technique in the Impact tactic. For this technique, and a large number of techniques in the network matrix, there are no sub-techniques. The point of exploiting public-facing applications is it's almost guaranteed that a company has at least a few public-facing applications. These could be websites, file servers, exchange servers, databases, or public-facing DNSes, to name a few. Exploiting those applications can sometimes lead to a further compromise of the internal network or could be used as a pivot point to attack other networks. APT28 used *CVE-2020-17144* and *CVE-2020-0688* to compromise exchange servers and APT39 used SQL injections to compromise public-facing applications belonging to a large number of organizations based out of the Middle East. For mitigation, it is critical to ensure that systems are updated and proper application isolation is put in place, and to implement a **Web Application Firewall** (**WAP**).

The next technique is Network Boundary Bridging within the Defense Evasion tactic, which is the action of joining networks together by compromising a permitter network device in order to bypass any IP or traffic restrictions. There is one sub-technique:

- *Network Address Translation Traversal*: A **Network Address Translation** (**NAT**) server maps multiple local private addresses to one public IP address. NAT traversal allows an attacker to maintain specific IP connections as they go through different gateways. This is used in peer-to-peer file sharing.

Network Boundary Bridging would allow an attacker to bypass security restrictions and traverse all segments of the network. They can also utilize NAT traversal to transfer malicious files to the network or endpoints. There are a few tools that can help Network Bounding Bridging and NAT traversal such as STUN, TURN, and ICE. For mitigation, you can ensure that MFA is enabled for authenticating to any network devices, that you filter and monitor network traffic, and that you have a robust password policy for any authentications. Detection is primarily based on alerting, so you can create detections to monitor network data to alert on an unusual network flow or create alerts on authentications to network devices based on locations or unusual times.

The next technique is Network Sniffing, which is under both the Credential Access and Discovery tactics. There are no sub-techniques. **Network Sniffing** is the action of reading network traffic packets as they flow on an active network. Some of the common tools for sniffing and analyzing network traffic are Wireshark, tcpdump, and TShark. What makes network sniffing so dangerous is that if unencrypted traffic is captured, an attack can collect credentials, extract files, or find reconnaissance information on any applications that are connected, sending traffic to the internet. A perfect example of the information that can be found is to go to any public network such as a hotel or coffee shop and start a packet capture and you'll be able to find all types of network traffic. This technique is commonly used in attempts to capture sensitive information as we have seen with groups such as APT28, APT33, and DarkVishnay. For mitigation steps, make sure all sensitive traffic is encrypted and requires authentication to access your network. For detection, implement alerts and monitoring processes that can be associated with network captures.

The next technique is System Information Discovery in the Discovery tactic and it has no sub-techniques. This is the process of getting detailed information such as hostnames, OSes and versions, and patches to be used for future targeted attacks against the network. In fact, this action directly relates to the reconnaissance phase of the Cyber Kill-Chain, which was discussed in *Chapter 4*. Almost every single APT group has used this technique and there are countless malware files and tools that provide this information. In fact, depending on how prevalent scanning is, most organizations don't bother with blocking external scanning because of how common it is. Since it is managed by the attacker and network traffic, there aren't many, if any, mitigation steps that can be taken because organizations need to do their own vulnerability scanning for best security practices. For detection, you would monitor network traffic to determine whether there is traffic that is attempting to retrieve information, but unless it is overly noisy and causing network problems, most of the traffic will go untouched.

The last technique is Traffic Signaling in the Persistence, Defense Evasion, and Command and Control tactics and it has one sub-technique:

- *Port Knocking*: This involves hiding open network ports in an attempt to mask the network traffic that is being sent to a C2 server in an attempt to evade detection. This is done by sending a set of attempts to closed ports and after the sequence is completed, opening a port on the firewall.

Traffic signaling as a whole is a process in which an attacker is attempting to open ports via a sequence, which could be attempted on closed ports, as is the case for Port Knocking, or it could be done using a set of specific network packets; it's the entrance of a magic key or sequence that allows you to configure specific settings. A form of malware that has used Traffic Signaling is the Ryuk Ransomware, which used it to take over machines to be able to spread, and the Pandora rootkit, which analyzes network packets; if the right sequence of packets is sent, it carries out the command. There are really only two steps for mitigation; the first is to monitor and alert your filtered network data for sequences and the second is to disable the Wake-on-LAN feature, which is the feature that the Ryuk Ransomware abused.

As you can tell from looking at the network matrix, most of the techniques vary significantly from some of the other matrices that we have analyzed, and most of the mitigation steps revolve around proper monitoring of network data. The other observation is that while it vaguely refers to some network devices such as permitter devices and public-facing applications, it goes nowhere near being in-depth and that would cause anyone to overlook it, but it still contains valuable information. Just be aware that you'll have to conduct research and review network traffic on your own to look at what other steps can be taken to mitigate risk within your network.

In the next section, we'll cover matrices that are associated with mobile devices since we are connected to our mobile devices every day.

A deep dive into the techniques in the mobile framework

We live in a connected world and it's rare to see a person without at least one mobile device. In our pockets, we have access to a ton of financial and personal information, not to mention that most of us also have access to our corporate networks. It's also a known factor that end users are considered one of the weakest links in an organization's security posture. That said, we understand that you can only recommend instead of apply security controls to end users with their personal phones, but you can protect your organization-owned mobile devices. One good thing about mobile devices is that there really are only iOS- and Android-based devices, so you don't have to factor in a ton of variations, just the base OSes and then the additional producers. In this section, we'll take a look at the overarching mobile matrix, the Android matrix, and the iOS matrix and pick out a few techniques to review. The mobile matrix looks like this:

- Initial Access
  - Drive-by Compromise, Lockscreen Bypass, Replication Through Removable Media, and Supply Chain Compromise

- Execution

    - Command and Scripting Interpreter, Native API, and Scheduled Task/Job

- Persistence

    - Boot or Logon Initialization Scripts, Compromise Application Executable, Compromise Client Software Binary, Event Triggered Execution, Foreground Persistence, Hijack Execution Flow, and Scheduled Task/Job

- Privilege Escalation

    - Abuse Elevation Control Mechanism, Exploitation for Privilege Escalation, and Process Injection

- Defense Evasion

    - Download New Code at Runtime, Execution Guardrails, Foreground Persistence, Hide Artifacts, Hooking, Impair Defenses, Indicator Removal on Host, Input Injection, Native API, Obfuscated Files or Information, Process Injection, Proxy Through Victim, Subvert Trust Controls, and Virtualization/Sandbox Evasion

- Credential Access

    - Access Notifications, Clipboard Data, Credentials from Password Store, Input Capture, and Steal Application Access Token

- Discovery

    - File and Directory Discovery, Location Tracking, Network Service Scanning, Process Discovery, Software Discovery, System Information Discovery, System Network Configuration Discovery, and System Network Connections Discovery

- Lateral Movement

    - Exploitation of Remote Services and Replication Through Removable Media

- Collection

    - Access Notifications, Adversary-in-the-Middle, Archive Collected Data, Audio Capture, Call Control, Clipboard Data, Data from Local System, Input Capture, Location Tracking, Protected User Data, Screen Capture, Stored Application Data, and Video Capture

- Command and Control

    - Application Layer Protocol, Call Control, Dynamic Resolution, Encrypted Channel, Ingress Tool Transfer, Non-Standard Port, Out of Band Data, and Web Service

- Exfiltration
  - Exfiltration Over Alternative Protocol and Exfiltration over C2 Channel

- Impact
  - Account Access Removal, Call Control, Data Encrypted for Impact, Data Manipulation, Endpoint Denial of Service, Generate Traffic from Victim, Input Injection, Network Denial of Service, and SMS Control

As you can see, there are a large number of techniques in the overall mobile matrix, and there are quite a few that are unique to mobile only. The first technique that we'll dig into is the Impair Defenses technique under the Defense Evasion tactic, which has three sub-techniques:

- *Prevent Application Removal*: This is completed by an attacker abusing the administrative features of a mobile device to not allow an end user to uninstall a potentially malicious application

- *Device Lockout*: This is the attacker locking the end user out of their mobile device so that they can access data without being interrupted

- *Disable or Modify Tools*: This is when the attacker exploits administrative privileges and disables diagnostic and security tools on a mobile device

Each of these sub-techniques and the technique as a whole is centered around the end user not having the ability to modify their mobile device once an initial compromise is made. Tools such as Anubia and Cerebus help enable attackers to carry out actions such as disabling Google Play Protect. Some mitigation steps vary depending on whether the mobile device is corporate-owned or private. For example, if it is a corporate device, the mobile device should be enrolled in a **Mobile Device Management** (**MDM**) scheme to manage all of the security settings and monitor for any suspicious activity. If it is a personal device, we recommend ensuring your mobile device's OS is up to date and installing security software. For detection options, end users have the ability to see what administrative tasks and privileges there are by reviewing the applications and device settings. Ensure that apps have the appropriate level of privileges.

The next technique we'll examine is the Protect User Data technique under the Collection tactic, which has four sub-techniques. The four sub-techniques are the following:

- *Calendar Entries*: An attacker would want to review calendar entries for any personal information such as locations, numbers, and points of contact, essentially information that can be used for potential social engineering

- *Call Log*: This is only applicable to Android devices, but an attacker would be able to leverage an Android API to review the call entries

- *Contact List*: APIs or frameworks on both iOS and Android could be leveraged to allow an attacker to see the full contact list, which could be valuable information for social engineering and spam

- *SMS Messages*: This is primarily on leveraging an Android API to read all text messages, which occasionally contain personal or sensitive information

> **Important note**
> One thing to keep in mind is that if you jailbreak your mobile device, you are much more susceptible to compromise.

The idea of protecting personal data should be a priority for everyone as that information can be used for potential future compromises, social engineering, or to target contacts. Some malware, such as the AndroRAT, has the ability to review text messages. The Corona Updates malware can collect and read a device's call logs. Steps for mitigation rely on not jailbreaking any devices, informing users about clicking on suspicious links, and downloading programs from unverified sites.

Next, we'll investigate the Android-specific matrix. There are approximately 2.5 billion Android users in the world, which makes it an incredibly large target, and security has to be taken into consideration. The Android matrix looks like this:

- Initial Access
  - Drive-by Compromise, Lockscreen Bypass, Replication Through Removable Media, and Supply Chain Compromise

- Execution
  - Command and Scripting Interpreter, Native API, and Scheduled Task/Job

- Persistence
  - Boot or Logon Initialization Scripts, Compromise Application Executable, Compromise Client Software Binary, Event Triggered Execution, Foreground Persistence, Hijack Execution Flow, and Scheduled Task/Job

- Privilege Escalation
  - Abuse Elevation Control Mechanism, Exploitation for Privilege Escalation, and Process Injection

- Defense Evasion
  - Download New Code at Runtime, Execution Guardrails, Foreground Persistence, Hide Artifacts, Hooking, Impair Defenses, Indicator Removal on Host, Input Injection, Native API, Obfuscated Files or Information, Process Injection, Proxy Through Victim, Subvert Trust Controls, and Virtualization/Sandbox Evasion

- Credential Access
  - Access Notifications, Clipboard Data, Input Capture, and Steal Application Access Token

- Discovery
  - File and Directory Discovery, Location Tracking, Network Service Scanning, Process Discovery, Software Discovery, System Information Discovery, System Network Configuration Discovery, and System Network Connections Discovery

- Lateral Movement
  - Exploitation of Remote Services and Replication Through Removable Media

- Collection
  - Access Notifications, Adversary in the Middle, Archive Collected Data, Audio Capture, Call Control, Clipboard Data, Data from Local System, Input Capture, Locations tracking, Protected User Data, Screen Capture, Stored Application Data, and Video Capture

- Command and Control
  - Application Layer Protocol, Call Control, Dynamic Resolution, Encrypted Channel, Ingress Tool Transfer, Non-Standard Port, Out of Band Data, and Web Service

- Exfiltration
  - Exfiltration Over Alternative Protocol and Exfiltration over C2 Channel

- Impact
  - Account Access Removal, Call Control, Data Encrypted for Impact, Data Manipulation, Endpoint Denial of Service, Generate Traffic from Victim, Input Injection, Network Denial of Service, and SMS Control

The first technique that we'll review is the Foreground Persistence control that is in both the Defense Evasion and Persistence tactics. There are no sub-techniques. **Foreground Persistence** is when a specific API, the `startForeground` one, is compromised, which allows an attacker to run on a device and load notifications as a legitimate application might do, which could allow for escalated permissions or to kill the Android's resources. Newer versions of Android have disabled the ability for idle applications to use the sensor data. The Mandrake malware specifically shows transparent notifications to allow its malware to remain persistent and evade detection. Unfortunately, the only step for mitigation that can be taken is to inform users about being careful as to what access and what permissions they grant.

The other technique that we'll review is the Screen Capture technique in the Collection tactic. This technique is special as it only applies to Android and not iOS. There are no sub-techniques. Screen Capture is carried out by an attacker utilizing the `screencap`, `screenrecord`, or `MediaProjectionManager` commands. If they were to be executed by an attacker, an attacker would be able to read contents, which could contain sensitive information such as passwords, personally identifiable information, and banking information. Some malware such as Anubis and Exodus can be used in this type of compromise. For mitigation, informing the end users on best security practices is a necessity and developers can apply the `Flag_Secure` setting property to their applications.

The last matrix that will be reviewed is the iOS one. While iOS has fewer users than Android, there are still over 900 million users. The iOS matrix looks like this:

- Initial Access
  - Drive-by Compromise, Lockscreen Bypass, Replication Through Removable Media, and Supply Chain Compromise

- Execution
  - Command and Scripting Interpreter and Scheduled Task/Job

- Persistence
  - Boot or Logon Initialization Scripts, Compromise by Client Software Binary, and Scheduled Task/Job

- Privilege Escalation
  - Exploitation for Privilege Escalation and Process Injection

- Defense Evasion
  - Download New Code at Runtime, Execution Guardrails, Indicator Removal on Host, Obfuscated Files or Information, Process Injection, Subvert Trust Controls, and Virtualization/Sandbox Evasion

- Credential Access
  - Clipboard Data, Credentials from Password Store, Input Capture, and Steal Application Access Token

- Discovery
  - File and Directory Discovery, Location Tracking, Network Service Scanning, Process Discovery, Software Discovery, System Information Discovery, and System Network Configuration Discovery

- Lateral Movement

  - Exploitation of Remote Services and Replication Through Removable Media

- Collection

  - Adversary in the Middle, Archive Collected Data, Audio Capture, Clipboard Data, Data from Local System, Input Capture, Locations tracking, Protected User Data, Stored Application Data, and Video Capture

- Command and Control

  - Application Layer Protocol, Dynamic Resolution, Encrypted Channel, Ingress Tool Transfer, Non-Standard Port, Out of Band Data, and Web Service

- Exfiltration

  - Exfiltration Over Alternative Protocol and Exfiltration over C2 Channel

- Impact

  - Endpoint Denial of Service, Generate Traffic from Victim, and Network Denial of Service

In this matrix, there are fewer techniques than the Android one but one thing that is interesting is that there are no unique techniques between the iOS and the Android matrices. The best practices for this matrix are to ensure that you download legitimate applications, know what the links you click on are, and don't jailbreak your device.

Mobile data as a whole is really important to remember to secure. It's a field that is only projected to continue to grow, as everything is connected digitally, and presents a large area for cyber risks. As covered, the mobile matrices are a great place to start when it comes to assessing the mobile risk for your organization and can be used to create a plan to implement mitigation and detection to make your organization more secure.

Summary

We looked at multiple different types of matrices within the MITRE ATT&CK framework, and keep in mind that there are regular updates to these in the form of changes to techniques, sub-techniques, and so on, so you'll want to periodically review the matrices to ensure that you are applying the latest information in your assessments.

In the next chapter, we'll cover how to actually apply the controls from the MITRE ATT&CK framework to your environment, so you can fuse your knowledge of the controls with some practical experience and work to implement some of the detection and monitoring steps within your own networks.

Strategies to Map to ATT&CK

In this chapter, we'll discuss how to analyze your environment, identify coverage gaps, and how to identify areas for improvement. Then, we'll cover how to map those gaps to the ATT&CK Framework to increase coverage and build out maturity in your security posture.

This chapter covers the following topics:

- Finding the gaps in your coverage
- Prioritization of efforts to increase efficiency
- Examples of mappings in real environments

Technical requirements

For this specific chapter, there is no specific technology or installations that are required.

Finding the gaps in your coverage

It's not logical to think that you can immediately review any/all controls from the MITRE ATT&CK Framework. Doing so will not only create a massive headache for yourself and your team but also could lead to adding unnecessary tools and leaving you trying to obtain the impossible. A perfect example is the **Actions on Objectives** control, which is complicated. The main principle is that there are various actions on an objective (actions taken against a target system such as a network or host) that can be carried out, such as stealing credentials, installing malware, and so on, but until an attack starts, you are unable to predict what is going to occur at some undetermined time in the future. In this case, you want to have a strong defense-in-depth approach by implementing standard security controls. Also, with regard to controls, it helps to understand that you will inevitably experience a compromise at some point in time if you haven't already. Technology is moving at a pace that is so fast and there are so many different factors that can impact your security that it is inevitable. What you can do is document your weaknesses and make a plan to mitigate as many as possible and hope that the controls that you have in place will protect you in the case of a catastrophic event.

The main approaches that my teams take to identify gaps are the use of purple team exercises, audits, and tabletop exercises, or the use of other commercial or open source tools. The first approach mentioned is **purple teams**, which as previously explained are collaborative efforts between a red team action (offense) and a blue team action (defense). They are needed when attacks are attempted to test response actions or security implementations and identify your weak spots. The weaknesses that are identified can be considered gaps, which you will add to your plan. The next approach is auditing. This can be aligned with any accreditation format that you have to follow, such as **Payment Card Industry Data Security Standard (PCI DSS)**, **Systems and Organizations Controls (SOC)**, the **Global Data Protection Regulation (GDPR)**, using the **Defense Information Systems Agency Security Technical Implementation Guide (DISA STIG)**, and so on. You can perform the audit internally or with a third party, which ensures you meet all controls to gain or maintain compliance. You can similarly do this with the MITRE ATT&CK Framework, but because the framework is not a compliance framework, it is more ambiguous. An example of the differences would be that DISA STIGs match specific systems, such as a STIG set for Windows Server 2019, and it tells you specifically where to go in the settings to ensure share drives cannot be enumerated. It looks like this:

Windows Server 2019 must not allow anonymous enumeration of shares.

Overview

Finding ID	Version	Rule ID	IA Controls	Severity
V-93537	WN19-SO-000230	SV-103623r1_rule		High

Description

Allowing anonymous logon users (null session connections) to list all account names and enumerate all shared resources can provide a map of potential points to attack the system.

STIG	Date
Windows Server 2019 Security Technical Implementation Guide	2020-06-15

Details

Check Text (C-92853r1_chk)

If the following registry value does not exist or is not configured as specified, this is a finding:

Registry Hive: HKEY_LOCAL_MACHINE
Registry Path: \SYSTEM\CurrentControlSet\Control\Lsa\

Value Name: RestrictAnonymous

Value Type: REG_DWORD
Value: 0x00000001 (1)

Fix Text (F-99781r1_fix)

Configure the policy value for Computer Configuration >> Windows Settings >> Security Settings >> Local Policies >> Security Options >> "Network access: Do not allow anonymous enumeration of SAM accounts and shares" to "Enabled".

Figure 6.1 – STIG viewer details of Windows Server 2019's findings

For this specific control, as depicted in the preceding figure, you can see the description, details, fix, and so on. Meanwhile, a tactic in the ATT&CK framework for the enumeration of shares can be found at **Network Share Discovery**, which is Tactic T1135 and looks like this:

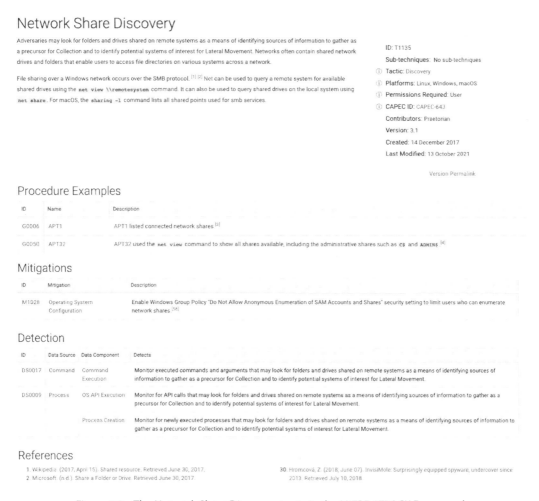

Figure 6.2 – The Network Share Discovery tactic in the MITRE ATT&CK Framework

As you can see, there is a lot of data provided in the MITRE tactic details, but it doesn't go to the granular level that something such as a STIG does. That's why it's helpful to run audits based on the compliance standard that you are compliant with and then map the non-compliant findings to the MITRE tactics. In fact, it's pretty easy to find resources online that have done this mapping for you, which helps take some of that guesswork out. The third approach mentioned was the use of tabletop exercises, which we covered in previous chapters, but as a reminder, these are exercises where you bring a group of stakeholders into a room and talk through a hypothetical incident. The pro to this is that you can pick out major gaps; however, this shouldn't be your only approach to findings gaps because it's easy to overlook technical controls or make assumptions about capabilities. If anything, it should be used for more assurance that your organization is doing the right thing. The last approach that was mentioned was to use tools that may either be commercial software offerings or open source tools. Tools such as SecurityScorecard, Splunk Security Essentials, Tripwire, and countless others map out your network through scanning, configurations, and so on and provide ratings for your security posture and let you know what areas need improvement. A pro of this approach is that it allows you to automate and check your security posture regularly, but a negative is that these tools usually take time to configure and don't account for compensating controls that might have been put in place. These tools can also display the findings in an easy-to-read and digestible format as follows:

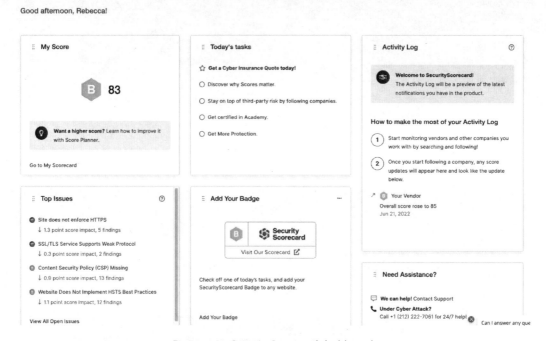

Figure 6.3 – SecurityScorecard dashboard

As you can see from the SecurityScorecard dashboard, just using the free version provides your security score and lists out the top issues that have been identified. This was set up within 5 minutes of registering for the free version and has provided findings. The gaps here appear to be around the website of the company that was registered, and the top issues found may be mapped to MITRE tactic T1600, **Weaken Encryption Technique**, due to HTTPS not being enforced.

The final approach that wasn't previously mentioned but is as important as purple team exercises, if not more, is to *trust your employees and coworkers*. Any SOC environment should strive to hire the best talent that they can, and many times, I've had employees approach me with gaps that they have identified through their experience or observations. You can then take a trust-but-verify approach of completing a proof of concept on the gap to ensure it is legitimate and then work together to map the respective gaps and mitigate them when possible. That way, you are incorporating a purple team approach and making that employee feel valued.

Regardless of what approach you take, you should try to match all gaps to MITRE to understand the risks associated with each gap, which can help with prioritization efforts when deciding what to remediate. You should also ensure to use a committee setup so other stakeholders can review the gaps and add their input, either adding mitigating controls, adding gaps, or agreeing to the proposed changes. All gaps should be reviewed, and if any are not going to be remediated, they should be added to your organizational risk registry for future tracking.

In the next section, we'll look at some strategies for prioritizing the gaps that have been identified and the approaches that make the most sense to your organization.

Prioritization of efforts to increase efficiency

Prioritization can be made using a variety of approaches, and it sometimes can come down to a feeling. For the record, when possible, you should use a quantitative method for prioritization, primarily based on capabilities. To start with, you need to have your gaps identified. That can be done through a risk registry, a purple team exercise, an audit, and so on. From there, you need to take a look at your resources; this includes the current technical capabilities, the personnel and their skill sets, the budget constraints to upgrade or bring in new tools and services, and the work cycles you have available or can make available. After you take a look at your resources, you want to then begin assigning prioritization and scoping out levels of effort, potential fixes, and stakeholders. One helpful tool is to diagram and actually write down the risks. If we were to step through a process, we could start with the following gaps:

Identified Gap	Tactics	Techniques	Risks	Likelihood	Impact	Stakeholders
Multi-Factor Authentication is Not Enabled	Credential Access	Unsecured Credentials, Modify Authentication Process	Could make accounts more susceptible to takeover and allow unauthorized access.	High	High	IT Admins
Limited Phishing Prevention Training	Initial Access	Phishing	An end user could click on a phishing link, resulting in actions such as downloading a malicious file or credential misuse.	High	Moderate/High	Endusers/IT Admins

Figure 6.4 – Identified gaps listed

From the example in the preceding figure, you can see that we have the gaps identified, what tactics and techniques they are related to, what some of the potential risks are, their likelihood and impact, and the stakeholders involved. This allows us to have a single point of reference for all gaps, as mentioned, like a **risk register**. The difference is that this will be used to add on columns and is for the prioritization of projects, whereas in my experience, risk registers are used for more long-term risk tracking and provide another way to prioritize gaps, depending on how you want to present the findings. If you're struggling with a way to match them up, one way is as an exercise for the entire team. You would use a four-quadrant chart and place a dot or title wherever a gap falls. The chart would look like this:

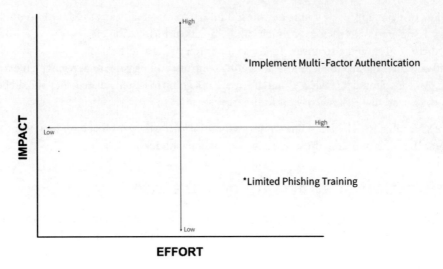

Figure 6.5 – Impact versus effort chart

As you can see from the preceding chart, you would mark where gap remediation would fall depending on the amount of impact it could have on the company if breached, and the amount of effort it would take to make the change. You could make this a collaborative effort by having all members of your team fill out their own chart and compare or create the single chart as a team. Regardless, there should be time built in to get feedback to ensure that all stakeholders agree on the general level of impact and effort needed to fill a gap.

A different way to prioritize might be based strictly on business needs. For example, if Company A is a provider of authentication services, and its gap is that it doesn't offer a centralized multi-factor authentication option, or that it doesn't enforce multi-factor authentication for privileged accounts, then that would be a higher priority than the phishing training. The reason is that if an authentication company has a compromise due to a lack of authentication protections, then it's a risk to the company, its customers' data, and its outward reputation, which enables it to continue to provide its services. While phishing training is important, other mitigating factors might be in place, so that gets pushed to the bottom of the priority list.

Similarly, if you feel your team needs some wins and you have enough business cycles, I would use a mixed approach. I would start with a lower-effort project, such as the phishing training, and work with a tool such as **KnowBe4** or create custom training to quickly push out phishing and cyber awareness training within the organization. I also recommend trying live tests through tools such as **gophish**, which you can use to send fake phishing emails to your workforce to test the click rate and assess the level of need for additional training, or even create smart groups so that when a user clicks on a fake phishing link, they are immediately enrolled into phishing training.

Regardless of the justification for prioritization, you'll want to gather contextual information that will be helpful. That's where including information such as the major milestones involved in the remediation and the stakeholders involved and tying this back to techniques and tactics can be extremely helpful. For example, by tying the gaps to tactics and techniques, you can use the resources provided by the MITRE ATT&CK Framework to help accurately assess the impact and likelihood of breaches. In the case of multi-factor authentication, you can see that it applies to the following techniques:

- **T1621**: Multi-Factor Authentication Request Generation
- **T1110**: Brute Force
- **T1111**: Multi-Factor Authentication Interception
- **T1098**: Account Manipulation
- **T1021**: Remote Services
- **T1199**: Trusted Relationship
- **T1136**: Create Account
- **T1530**: Data from Cloud Storage
- **T1213**: Data from information Repositories: Code Repositories
- **T1114**: Email Collection
- **T1133**: External Remote Services
- **T1556**: Modify Authentication Process
- **T1601**: Modify System Image
- **T1599**: Network Boundary Bridging
- **T1040**: Network Sniffing
- **T1072**: Software Deployment Tools
- **T1539**: Steal Web Session Cookie
- **T1078**: Valid Accounts (Domain and Cloud)

Primarily, multi-factor authentication ensures that only those authorized are able to authenticate and access specific resources, which is important, but it can also be helpful for mitigating credential stuffing and other brute-force attacks. As you can see, there are a large number of tactics that are related to multi-factor authentication, which is why it's important to completely map tactics to the gaps when possible. Effectively doing so will allow you to accurately assess the level of effort and impact that that gap involves and can allow you to properly prioritize your work.

Speaking with a colleague recently, they chose to prioritize operations that had synergy first. The reason is that you can potentially knock out multiple initiatives at once because some of them will require the same or similar steps to be taken. They found that by lining up gaps by synergy, they were able to optimize their team and make a greater short-term impact and then work on a plan to figure out the separate gaps and decide with their respective teams on what could and could not be remediated.

In the next section, I'll talk through a few different cases of a hypothetical scenario and how we would map it to the related tactics. After all of them are mapped, I'll walk through how I would prioritize the efforts.

Examples of mappings in real environments

Security vulnerabilities and coverage gaps are a fact of life for anyone who works in infosec. Here are a few different outlined security coverage issues that I've experienced and their applicable mapping and prioritization on a quad chart, as well as a discussion about what work streams I would implement. All of these issues are extremely common and hopefully can provide insight for you as you look at your environment.

The first issue that I've run into multiple times is a lack of logging, or a lack of logging the proper security logs. The reason that this is a problem is that logs are the first place a security responder will look when investigating an alert and attempting to find anything that is suspicious or malicious. If logging is not up to par, there are likely compromised activities occurring that you are not aware of because logs are also typically used to set up detection and alerts. To identify whether this is an issue, you need to determine what logs you need to capture based on the infrastructure and work structure of your organization. You also want to project out the size of the logs that you want to ingest into your log correlation tool. That way, you can assign priority to the missing logs. I assign my logs priority based on the number of potential detection rules and the level of effort needed to ingest them. For example, a list of missing logs might look like this:

Data Source	Vendor	Product	Priority	Relative Size	2023 GB	Notes
Zero-Trust VPN	OpenVPN	OpenVPN	Critical	Extra Large	500	
Authentication	One Identity	OneLogin	Critical	Large	115	
Cloud Security	AWS	Guard Duty	Moderate	Medium	50	
Vulnerability Scans	Tenable	Nessus	Low	Small	10	

Figure 6.6 – Log source organization

As you can see, I've created a table that has the list of data sources that I want added to ingest, the vendor the sources come from (this matters when you have to determine potential integrations), the specific product the logs are coming from, the priority, the size based off of an internal scale, the size in the form of project GB for the next year, and a section for any additional notes. I would then be able to take this list and work with the respective teams to either implement integration or forwarders for ingesting logs. Even then, it's not quite that simple because you have to take into consideration costs and technical constraints. The number one reason I have experienced limited logging is due to cost, as some SIEM tools can be cost-prohibitive as you ingest more data, which isn't reasonable for a smaller organization to pay for. If that's the case, and you have the bandwidth for management, you should look into using an open source solution, such as standing up an **Elastic, Logstash,** and **Kibana (ELK)** stack.

Now, how does limited logging map to MITRE? In quite a few areas. Depending on the data, in this case, we'll use some of the examples from the chart of missing zero-trust VPN logs, authentication logs, guard duty logs, and vulnerability scans; they could be mapped to the following tactics:

- **T1133**: External Remote Services
- **T1021**: Remote Services
- **T1570**: Lateral Tool Transfer
- **T1078**: Valid Accounts
- **T1098**: Account Manipulation
- **T1046**: Network Service Discovery

These are just a few that could potentially be mapped to the missing logs. It of course would depend on the level of configuration that you have for the various tools as to other ones that could be mapped. In general, I find it easier to identify all of the tactics that could apply, and that determines which ones have coverage for mitigation and other implementations. That way, I don't accidentally leave one out of the potential list.

Another common security flaw that I have found at smaller companies was a lack of security training or immature security training. In general, I recommend yearly training, on top of exercises such as phishing exercises to test the employee group, so that everyone can become cyber-smart. Some controls that could relate to the lack of training could be as follows:

- **T1566**: Phishing Spearphishing Link
- **T1598**: Phishing for Information
- **T1550**: Use Alternate Authentication Material
- **T1098**: Account Manipulation

In this case, phishing tactics are obvious to map to security awareness training. However, other tactics were mentioned, which shows that training has a far reach. For example, if there are no procedures and no training on security, then what is keeping an administrator from granting overly permissive permissions or adding different methods of authentication because they might not understand the consequences? This shows that when mapping, you need to keep an open mind and try to understand the blast radius of an attack.

The third security flaw that I have seen is that **Access Control Lists (ACLs)** might be open to the internet or at least less restrictive than they should be. This is a common area, especially in development teams, where instances are stood up and down. It's easier to leave the instance open to the internet than taking the time to restrict it due to the thought that it'll get torn down quickly, or is just an oversight. I have worked on multiple incidents in my career, even early on, caused by shadow instances that had overly permissive ACLs, and given the move of practically everything to the cloud, this will only continue to occur. Some tactics that could be mapped to this finding are as follows:

- **T1069**: Permission Groups Discovery
- **T1046**: Network Service Discovery
- **T1557**: Adversary in the Middle
- **T1563**: Remote Service Session Hijacking

Again, these are just a few of the tactics that could apply, and if you have an overly permissive ACL and weak authentication, then you are at a higher risk for an overall compromise, which would be detrimental to your organization.

Taking these three security areas into account and thinking about work streams, I would categorize them on a quad chart as follows:

Figure 6.7 – Prioritization quad chart

As you can see on this chart, I placed logging at high-effort/high-impact, placed ACLS as mostly high-effort and mostly high-impact, and placed security training as low- to mid-effort with a moderate impact. I chose these designations because implementing logging will take significant effort via creating integration or setting up forwarders, and that's if you even have the bandwidth on your tool to ingest the additional logs. The logs do provide a significant amount of impact because of the visibility they provide and the detections that can be created based on the logs. The ACLs involve moderate to high effort because they will need monitoring solutions, the likes of **Guard Duty**, **Twistlock**, or other tools. Policy creation will be needed to determine the proper ways to stand up instances and training. It is also ranked as having a moderate to high impact because of my experience with how common a security flaw this is, and having worked on multiple incidents in the past that were a result of this. Security training is placed as low to moderate in terms of both effort and impact. For effort, it's because there are a large number of solutions that can be implemented to easily assign and manage security training, and while there is a large amount of effort to set it up, you can coast to an extent (depending on your organization). In terms of impact, I am a big believer in training. However, it alone is not enough, and more needs to be done to protect your workforce. You may agree or disagree with the placements, but any placement is dependent on your organizational priorities.

For work streams, I would start implementing strong ACLs because I believe that will have the greatest impact-to-effort ratio. I think there is also synergy between implementing the ACLs and training, as in, training end users to set up proper ACLs. This shows that even though the logging project has a higher impact, it isn't the first one worked on in the work streams because of the amount of effort it involves, and the amount of discovery that would need to occur. If anything, it would make sense to start with implementing smaller, more accessible sources while scoping out larger sources.

Summary

As you can see, some of the concepts we've learned previously, such as purple team exercises and threat modeling, can all play a role when it comes to prioritization and mapping tactics to gaps. As you'll continue to see, security, in general, is interconnected, which means that when processes and teams work in synergy, then you are more likely able to implement a defense-in-depth approach to make your organization more secure. In the next chapter, we'll continue to talk through implementation and examine some of the mistakes that get made when implementing securing infrastructure and processes. I'll also walk through some of my previously failed security projects to go through what the lessons learned from those experiences were and what I would do differently if I were to complete those projects again.

7

Common Mistakes with Implementation

Mistakes happen; that's just a part of life. This chapter will provide an overview of common mistakes I have made in mappings and detections, as well as areas where I've seen others make mistakes. That way, you can learn from our shortcomings and implement mappings the right way.

The chapter will cover the following topics:

- Examples of incorrect technique mappings from ATT&CK
- Examples of poor executions with detection creation

Technical requirements

For this specific chapter, no installations or specific technologies are required.

Examples of incorrect technique mappings from ATT&CK

Mistakes happen, and we all know this. It could be an implementation that doesn't work, a lack of knowledge or direction, or a simple mistake that happened purely by accident. The problem is mistakes can have consequences of different sizes, and you don't typically know what the consequences are until they've already occurred. Hopefully, you can learn from some of the mistakes made in our past and use this to make your organization more secure.

For the first example, I think of times when I have tried to overextend resources to cover as many controls as possible, even when it wasn't likely to be successful. It was a common practice for a while to review any areas and try to implement detection, mitigation, and security controls without thinking of the consequences for the organization, and in the long run, that was an important lesson to learn. It might have started small with over-portioning user access controls to the point that some admin users had four or five different accounts, and the thought process was that there was the separation of duties with the accounts, making it more secure. The reality was that this resulted in very few people using them correctly. I would see a mixture of scenarios. One would be that all the accounts were created but not used, and a single admin account would be used. Another scenario was that passwords or pins would be the same across all accounts. Overall, it led to just as many, if not more, security issues and resentment built up toward the security and auditing teams. As having separate admin accounts that corresponded with roles was poorly implemented, we had to put in place stronger mitigations to ensure that there were proper privileged account management mitigations. Mismanagement of privileged access accounts can correlate to the following MITRE controls:

- **T1548**: Abuse Elevation Control Mechanism
  - Bypass User Account Control
  - Sudo and Sudo Caching
- **T1134**: Access Token Manipulation
  - Token Impersonation/Theft
  - Create Process with Token
  - Make and Impersonate Token
- **T1098**: Account Manipulation
  - Additional Cloud Credentials
  - Additional Email Delegate Permissions
  - Additional Cloud Roles
- **T1547**: Boot or Logon Autostart Execution: Kernel Modules and Extensions
- **T1612**: Build Image on Host
- **T1059**: Command and Scripting Interpreter
  - PowerShell
  - Network Devices CLI
- **T1609**: Container Administration Command
- **T1136**: Create Account
  - Local Account
  - Domain Account
  - Cloud Account
- **T1543**: Create or Modify System Process: Systemd Service

- **T1484**: Domain Policy Modification

  - Domain Trust Modification

- **T1611**: Escape to Host

- **T1546**: Event-Triggered Execution: Windows Management Instrumentation Event Subscription

- **T1190**: Exploit Public-Facing Application

- **T1210**: Exploitation of Remote Services

- **T1222**: File and Directory Permissions Modification

  - Windows File and Directory Permissions Modification

  - Linux and Mac File and Directory Permissions Modification

- **T1495**: Firmware Corruption

- **T1606**: Forge Web Credentials

  - SAML Tokens

- **T1562**: Impair Defenses: Safe Mode Boot

- **T1525**: Implant Internal Image

- **T1056**: Input Capture: Web Portal Capture

- **T1559**: Inter-Process Communication

  - Component Object Model

- **T1556**: Modify Authentication Process

  - Domain Controller Authentication

  - Pluggable Authentication Modules

  - Network Device Authentication

  - Reversible Encryption

  - Hybrid Identity

- **T1601**: Modify System Image

  - Patch System Image

  - Downgrade System Image

- **T1599**: Network Boundary Bridging

  - Network Address Translation Traversal

- **T1003**: OS Credential Dumping

  - LSASS Memory

  - Security Account Manager

  - NTDS

  - LSA Secrets

  - Cached Domain Credentials

  - DCSync

  - Proc Filesystem

  - `/etc/passwd` and `/etc/shadow`

- **T1542**: Pre-OS Boot

  - System Firmware

  - Bootkit

  - TFTP Boot

- **T1055**: Process Injection

  - Ptrace System Calls

- **T1563**: Remote Service Session Hijacking

  - SSH Hijacking

  - RDP Hijacking

- **T1021**: Remote Services

  - Remote Desktop Protocol

  - SMB/Windows Admin Shares

  - Distributed Component Object Model

  - Windows Remote Management

- **T1053**: Scheduled Task/Job

  - At

- Scheduled Task
- Systemd Timers
- Container Orchestration Job

- **T1505**: Server Software Component

  - SQL Stored Procedures
  - Transport Agent
  - IIS Components

- **T1072**: Software Deployment Tools

- **T1558**: Steal or Forge Kerberos Tickets

  - Golden Tickets
  - Silver Tickets
  - Kerberoasting

- **T1553**: Subvert Trust Controls: Code Signing Policy Modification

- **T1218**: System Binary Proxy Execution

  - Msiexec

- **T1569**: System Services

  - System Execution

- **T1552**: Unsecured Credentials

  - Credentials in Registry
  - Container API

- **T1550**: Use Alternate Authentication Material

  - Pass the Hash
  - Pass the Ticket

- **T1078**: Valid Accounts

  - Domain Accounts
  - Local Accounts
  - Cloud Accounts

- **T1047**: Windows Management Instrumentation

As you can see from that long list, privilege access management can be related to a large number of different techniques and sub-techniques, spanning different matrices and tactics. In creating the different admin accounts, the team implementing the access controls was so focused on being compliant with every **security technical implementation guide** (**STIG**) at the time that they weren't practical. If I were to go back in time, I would then recommend that team take the list of the MITRE techniques, filter out the ones for matrices that don't apply, and then compare the various mitigation and detection tips to make the account changes that would have the most impact. In this case, the practical response would be to have a separate end user and admin account or have a way to temporarily grant admin permissions based on the use case and have sufficient logging enabled to be able to review for misuse. This solution can be done in various ways, for example, using tools such as Allowance, which can grant admin access to authorized users for 24 hours. Again, this is one solution that I've used in environments in the past, and not all solutions to mistaken mappings will work for you.

Another scenario where we clearly over-complicated work instead and ended up creating more problems by not mapping and implementing controls in a way that made sense was a few years ago when we expanded our network detection and response capabilities. To do so, we needed to increase visibility. We essentially took on too many steps of utilizing a network defense and response tool, implementing SSL Decrypt for most traffic, and creating our own alerts, among other steps. At first glance, all of this sounds good; it provides visibility and alerting, but we had half-implemented projects because we were trying to do too much at once. For example, SSL Decrypt works if you are on the company network or the company VPN but we found that most users used their personal devices to conduct work unless absolutely necessary to be on their company endpoints. Similarly, we spread ourselves too thin by creating alerts, resulting in higher levels of false positives. Then, even when SSL Decrypt was put in place, many categories for data were not decrypted, and we would see malicious traffic use those categories fraudulently to ensure their traffic was still encrypted. That also rendered some of the alerts useless. Our strategy of doing as much as possible because the MITRE Framework can relate to the mitigation for the following techniques and sub-techniques:

- **T1557**: Adversary-in-the-Middle

  - LLMNR/NBT-NS Poisoning and SMB Relay

  - ARP Caching Poisoning

  - DHCP Spoofing

- **T1071**: Application Layer Protocol

  - Web Protocols

  - File Transfer Protocols

  - Mail Protocols

  - DNS

- **T1132**: Data Encoding
  - Standard Encoding
  - Non-Standard Encoding
- **T1602**: Data from Configuration Repository
  - SNMP (MIB Dump)
  - Network Device Configuration Dump
- **T1001**: Data Obfuscation
  - Junk Data
  - Steganography
  - Protocol Impersonation
- **T1030**: Data Transfer Size Limits
- **T1568**: Dynamic Resolution
  - Domain Generation Algorithms
- **T1573**: Encrypted Channel
  - Symmetric Cryptography
  - Asymmetric Cryptography
- **T1048**: Exfiltration Over Alternative Protocol
  - Exfiltration Over Symmetric Encrypted Non-C2 Protocol
  - Exfiltration Over Asymmetric Encrypted Non-C2 Protocol
  - Exfiltration Over Unencrypted Non-C2 Protocol
- **T1041**: Exfiltration Over C2 Channel
- **T1008**: Fallback Channels
- **T1105**: Ingress Tool Transfer
- **T1570**: Lateral Tool Transfer
- **T1104**: Multi-Stage Channels
- **T1046**: Network Service Discovery
- **T1095**: Non-Application Layer Protocol

- **T1571**: Non-Standard Ports
- **T1566**: Phishing

  - Spearphishing Attachment

- **T1542**: Pre-OS Boot

  - ROMMONkit

  - TFTP Boot

- **T1572**: Protocol Tunneling
- **T1090**: Proxy

  - Internal Proxy

  - External Proxy

- **T1219**: Remote Access Software
- **T1029**: Scheduled Transfer
- **T1221**: Template Injection
- **T1204**: User Execution

  - Malicious Link

  - Malicious Image

- **T1102**: Web Service

  - Dead Drop Resolver

  - Bidirectional Communication

  - One-Way Communication

Looking over the list of mitigations (and there are even more), when it comes to implementing network detection and response efforts, you can clearly tell that there are a lot of areas that can add value in the realm of making your environment more secure, but trying to attempt all types of mitigation at once doesn't make sense and, if anything, leads to you having your attention divided to the point where you are more likely to miss something or make a mistake with implementing the tools or even choosing tools that aren't the best for your environment. Instead, ensure that you analyze the controls you want to be implemented, determine how to create the mitigations and detections, then prioritize them so you don't try to tackle too many at once.

You should always strive to have common sense security measures in place because if you create controls that consistently make work harder, fewer and fewer people are going to follow those controls, but if you create controls that will change some workflows, don't add too much pain, and can get the point across about them through demonstrative security, then more people are likely to follow them. You also want to prioritize what controls you need to focus on and then make a plan based on the level of effort, the implementation, and potential pitfalls. A comprehensive plan will lead to a higher level of success for correct mapping to techniques and a higher level of success for correct implementation.

Examples of poor executions with detection creation

Creating alerts is part of any **security operations center** (**SOC**) team's responsibilities. That allows them to use Yara, **Splunk Processing Language** (**SPL**), Suricata, and so on, whatever language makes sense for the tools that your organization uses. I can also guarantee that anyone who has ever worked in a SOC can relate to having alerts that were created that just generate a large number of false positives and can quickly become tiresome to triage, or that, due to ineffective filtering on alerts, become quite complicated due to having more information than is needed. A few alerts come to mind, but the first one is an alert for **periodic beaconing**, which can be indicative of an infected system sending a ping out to a C2 server. This alert would/could map to the following techniques in MITRE:

- **T1071**: Application Layer Protocol

    - Web Protocols

    - File Transfer Protocols

    - Mail Protocols

    - DNS

- **T1132**: Data Encoding

    - Standard Encoding

    - Non-Standard Encoding

- **T1001**: Data Obfuscation

    - Junk Data

    - Steganography

    - Protocol Impersonation

This specific alert produced some positive results, but it also produced many false positives because of the nature of how some software works. This was especially pertinent with this alert triggering on Google Analytics and the company Instart (acquired by Akamai), which use beaconing-type traffic to gather information for search engine optimization. This would cause no less than 20 alerts a day, and even at 4 minutes per alert, that equates to almost an hour and a half of an analyst's time every day and can be broken down to a salary cost of $54 a day for an analyst that makes a salary of $75,000 a year, or a yearly cost of $14,062 a year. Of course, as you triage the same alert, you get more efficient and faster, but imagine if you had five alert rules such as this and the cost it could have on your business. The non-monetary cost is that while you're closing those alerts, you could be missing a more serious alert, and that could also have a large impact on your organization. At the same time, you can use those false positives to tune alerts and help make them better. In the case of this specific alert, we provided feedback to the detection engineering team and created processes to help speed up responding to repeatable false positives. If I could go back in time, I would also look to either write a script or integrate with a **Security Orchestration Automation Response** (**SOAR**) tool to automate closure after running through a set of checks in a run book.

Another alert is one that we used to cover large amounts of data transfers and their corresponding ports or to removable media such as USBs, which is for the following techniques:

- **T1020**: Automated Exfiltration

  - Traffic Duplication

- **T1030**: Data Transfer Size Limits

- **T1048**: Exfiltration Over Alternative Protocol

  - Exfiltration Over Symmetric Encrypted Non-C2 Protocol

  - Exfiltration Over Asymmetric Encrypted Non-C2 Protocol

  - Exfiltration Over Unencrypted Non-C2 Protocol

- **T1041**: Exfiltration Over C2 Channel

- **T1011**: Exfiltration Over Other Network Medium

  - Exfiltration Over Bluetooth

- **T1052**: Exfiltration Over Physical Medium

  - Exfiltration Over USB

- **T1567**: Exfiltration Over Web Service

  - Exfiltration to Code Repository

  - Exfiltration to Cloud Storage

- **T1029**: Scheduled Transfer

- **T1537**: Transfer Data to Cloud Account

We started off using Splunk and writing a simple alert:

```
index=network_data size= (bytes_out/1024) size>= 100 | table _time,
user, size
```

That SPL shows that we are looking at the indexed data from the network index. We create a variable for `size` that is `bytes out` divided by `1024` to show the size in kilobytes and whether the transfer is larger than `100` kilobytes. It then matches that string and puts it into a table format sorted by the timestamp for the data, the user, and the size of the transfer. This isn't the exact alert we used, but it gives you an idea. The issue with this and similar types of alerts is that it is way too vague. Data transfers can be completely legitimate most of the time, but the need for the alert also depends on factors such as your organization's acceptable use policy and the level of concern. While some transfers can download something as simple as a video clip or images for a presentation, I've also seen cases where entire code bases have been saved to an external drive, which someone can take when leaving the company. Regardless, in the attempt to make the alert more specific, you would want to add terms to continue to search on filtered-down data or separate alerts. For example, instead of generating alerts for all data transfer, you could have an alert that is specific to USBs or add in additional search terms or exclude terms such as specific IPs or websites that transfers occur from. Taking those steps will help you get a more efficient alert, which will allow you to figure out what occurred in a timely manner. You do need to be careful when tuning because it's an easy trap to fall into to just add on singular search filters such as IP addresses one by one, and before you know it, you'll have an SPL query that is six lines long (this has 100% happened to me). Instead, audit your alerts and look for ways to make them more efficient, which will also help use less processing power.

Summary

Mistakes regarding implementation and detection are bound to happen; not only have they already occurred but they will continue. The key is to learn from those mistakes, and you can then use that to be more prepared for the next implementation or learn to be more efficient when creating detections. You also shouldn't be ashamed to talk about failed projects because you can use that to get feedback and helpful suggestions from other industry professionals. Many times in my career, I'll talk through a particularly tough task and use my network to help talk through ideas.

In the next chapter, we'll discuss the alerts that, in my experience, have provided the most value. We'll also talk through ways to measure the efficacy of alerts and set up feedback loops to identify what alerts need to be improved.

8

Return on Investment Detections

Creating detections and alerts is the bread and butter of any **security operations center (SOC)** environment. It should not be a surprise to anyone that less than stellar detections are created/triggered daily. This chapter will discuss alerts that we have had the highest efficiency ratings on, as well as the lowest, and how to measure their success. The skills from this chapter will allow you to identify detections that are not efficient, create more efficient alerts, and implement metrics to measure alerts. The topics that we will cover in this chapter include:

- Reviewing examples of poorly created detections and their consequences
- Finding the winners or the best alerts
- Measuring the success of a detection

Technical requirements

For this specific chapter, no installations or specific technologies are required.

Reviewing examples of poorly created detections and their consequences

Detections are created to help fill a security gap, enforce a security policy, and align with a compliance standard, among other reasons. I'd like to say that every detection created is thought through carefully, modeled, and then created with optimization in mind, but that really isn't the case. The reality is that many alerts are created as a reactive action, so in response to a type of incident or a failed control of an audit. Then, you put in the simplest form of detection and go from there. A lot of the time, you forget about it unless it's overly noisy with false positives. The detections can have some true positives but usually cause more work than is necessary to weed through the alerts until you get to the point where you have to implement automation or tuning alerts.

The first detection that comes to my mind when I think of poorly created ones was done out of necessity and could not have been improved upon. The detection was created to alert about potential credit card data and other **personally identifiable information (PII)** theft. It essentially used a regular expression to alert about 16-digit numeric characters after searching different text documents and logs. In theory, it had the ability to work; however, it created a large number of false positives, which can eat up some of the triage time. It is an alert that, when it works, is important and provides value, and many tools have sample syntax to implement this type of alert. We also looked at plain text credentials in Splunk, and while similarly, this alert had findings, it also had missed detections and false positives. After some tuning, we were able to come up with the syntax in the following screenshot:

```
index=splunkConf (source IN("*.txt","*.log"))
| rex max_match=0
{ | inputlookup rainbow_table type="regex"
| eval rexValue="(?<T_"+replace(value, " ")>""+Test")"
| stats values(rexValue) AS regexMerge
| eval regexMerge=mvjoin(regexMerge,"|")
| fields search }
....
| where isnotnull(PatternStringMatch)
```

Figure 8.1 – Splunk syntax for plain text credentials

This alert, specifically as shown, looks into text and log files and compares them to a lookup table, which has common and default passwords. It then uses **regular expressions (regexes)** to search and find matches to alert on. This version of the detection is after a fair amount of tuning. If this detection was effective, it would apply to the following *MITRE* controls:

- **T1552**: Unsecured Credentials
  - Credentials in Files
  - Credentials in Registry
- **T1078**: Valid Accounts
  - Default Accounts

Another type of detection that I used in the past that was poorly written was to look for detections of large file transfers. For this to work, we used a simple alert:

```
Index=Splunk_Index_Name bytes_out=1000000
```

Essentially all the alert did was search for large files in our network logs that were being sent from endpoints, and it was one of the first alerts I looked at implementing in one of my first SOC environments. The purpose was for us to provide coverage for the following MITRE techniques, among others:

- **T1005**: Data from Local System
- **T1025**: Data from Removable Media
- **T1048**: Exfiltration Over Alternative Protocol

  - Exfiltration Over Asymmetric Encrypted Non-C2 Protocol
  - Exfiltration Over Unencrypted Non-C2 Protocol

- **T1041**: Exfiltration Over C2 Channel
- **T1052**: Exfiltration Over Physical Medium

  - Exfiltration over USB

- **T1567**: Exfiltration Over Web Service

We very quickly realized how ineffective this alert was because it alerted us about so many normal actions, such as emailing legitimate files and uploads to Google Docs; in one case, it was even triggered by an interior design picture. Even after tuning, we decided to stop this alert and focus on transfers to removable media until we could find time for further tuning. We did eventually tune the alert and turn it back on, and in Splunk, it looked like this:

```
index=splunkconf sourcetype=meraki OR (tag=web
tag=proxy) OR (sourcetype=email)

| where bytes_out>50000000
| eval megabytes=((bytes/1024)/1024)
| table _time src_ip user megabytes app url
```

Figure 8.2 – Large data transfers over network logs

As you can see, this alert takes the original poor detection and builds from it. First, it specifies the specific source type or tags in the index that we are looking for, which is network data from our Meraki devices, and data tagged with web, proxy, or email. This helped us run a more efficient search. Then, for our search terms, we looked for anything equal to or more than 50 MB, (50,000,000 bytes over 1,024 over 1,024). We then put all of the search results into an easily readable table format to quickly review our results. This version of the alert is not only more efficient in its search terms but is also conducted in a way where an analyst can quickly review the findings and have a more effective triage time.

Poor detections will always be around, especially with the first iteration of alerts. While they cause headaches by being ineffective, they provide you with a great learning opportunity to learn more about your environment by tuning and becoming more efficient at creating alerts. You should always look to use community resources and reach out for input and help from the information security community, so you can learn from their experiences and find what detections have been the most important for them. Now that we've looked at a couple of examples of bad detections, we can discuss some of the successful detections that I've had, in the next section.

Finding the winners or the best alerts

Anytime that you have an alert that proves successful and does so a higher percentage of the time (even 30% is exciting), it feels like you have a win. Those are the alert types that have always made me personally excited to triage and you want to find a way to continue that feeling and expand it to other detections. In my opinion, there are a few different categorizations for winning alerts. There is one where the alert is almost always going to be something actionable, whether it just shows a poor security practice, a violation of your acceptable use policy, or something more serious that could lead to an incident investigation starting. Then, there is an alert that is technically a true positive, but there are limited actions that can be taken. Finally, there are the surprise true positive alerts, which leave your team scrambling to triage and put together contextual information.

The first categorization can be all different alerts, but the first ones that I think about are cloud security-related. It starts with alerts that are generated when overly permissive security groups are created. These are security groups that have rules that are open to anything, so *0.0.0.0 rules* (which means that there are no IP restrictions), which could relate to the following techniques:

- **T1562**: Impair Defenses

  - Disable or Modify Cloud Firewall

- **T1040**: Network Sniffing
- **T1213**: Data from Information Repositories

  - Code Repositories

- **T1078**: Valid Accounts

  - Cloud Accounts

These are just a few of the techniques that could apply to this type of finding. Similarly, if an Amazon **Simple Storage Service** (**S3**) bucket or another piece of cloud infrastructure is left with the 0.0.0.0 rule, it could lead to unintentional access and information disclosure, and have a real impact on your business. Fortunately, creating this detection is fairly straightforward, depending on the type of architecture and cloud tools used. If you are using AWS, you can enable **GuardDuty**, which has this detection, or you could ingest logs from AWS or other cloud management tools such as **Twistlock** (now **Prisma Cloud**) and create detections within your log correlation tools such as Splunk. The beauty of this alert is that when it is triggered, you almost always have something actionable, and the majority of the time, in my experience, it's just an instance stood up for testing that is forgotten or a mistake, but that type of shadow IT is just plain poor security practices and can lead to an incident. So instead, if possible, all instances should be stood up from a golden image, or at the very least, restricted access controls should be in place.

An example of an alert when triggers are a true positive but could just signal business as usual for cloud environments is when resources are deleted; that way you can ensure that any records have been deleted, and proper procedure was covered. I have experienced cases in the past where there has been a partial deletion, but the records still exist in **Route 53**; this is a scalable **Domain Name System** (**DNS**) service that AWS uses. Records may still exist after an instance is deleted, and could lead to potential DNS spoofing and other types of DNS attacks. While this alert can be generated from GuardDuty, it is typically due to authorized action. Because this alert is triggered by an action, in general, it fires off as a true positive, so there is technically a high efficacy rate, but often requires a quick check to make sure it was an authorized deletion via looking at service tickets or talking with administrators. This also can relate to the following MITRE techniques, among others:

- **T1530**:Data from Cloud Storage
- **T1565**: Data Manipulation
  - Stored Data Manipulation

You can find out more about GuardDuty from AWS at this link: `https://aws.amazon.com/guardduty/`. If you are capturing *CloudTrail* logs, you'll be able to create the majority of the detections yourself. However, there are benefits to using GuardDuty if you don't have VPC Flow Logs enabled, even if there is an additional cost.

In general, you want to look for detections and alerts that cause an action, even if it is not malicious or is a misconfiguration. The better your efficacy rating, the more value you'll get out of it, which will help determine the metrics that will be used to tell your detect-and-respond story. In the next section, we'll cover how to measure the success of detection through key metrics.

Measuring the success of a detection

Measuring success is a key part of any organization, and SOCs, while they are operational, are no different. I've run SOC environments in a few different ways; primarily there is a split 60/40 of alert triage to project work. Project work can be anything from creating detections and runbooks to assisting with an audit or ingesting new log sources. Of course, that split is also variable based on incidents. Regardless, finding the right way to measure is key to determining success for both your SOC and detection.

Requirement-setting

The project aspect is straightforward on whether the project is completed or not. For that, I run quarterly sprints where our projects are broken down using business-driven development language or that of *Cucumber*, an open source software tool that can assist with writing test cases in a broken-down, non-technical format. An example of a ticket would be as follows:

"I'd like to ingest Microsoft Active Directory logs to gain visibility in our Active Directory environment so that we can create more security-based detections for user privileges and account actions."

Each ticket can be broken down into this type of language so there are logical steps and everyone understands the ask of the ticket. The ticket is then voted on as a group, with me, as the manager, having veto power to determine how many points or effort of work it is. A common point system is to use the Fibonacci sequence for points, so 1, 3, 5, 7 to determine the level of effort, and it is a collaborative effort to come to that agreement. A different point system is to equate each point to a number of hours and allocate points based on the number of work hours that cycle. The pointing system ensures that work is evenly spread across your team and gives you a measurable form for success with the project work. For detections, it's about finding measurements that work for you.

Most environments are historically configured to use connections, so when an alert triggers in **security information and event management** (**SIEM**), it automatically creates a ticket in the case management system. So, for example, a Splunk alert triggers, and a Jira ticket is created. The ticket is part of a queue system for all alerts so that triaging analysts can pick them up and have an area to keep any closure notes or escalate them to an incident. During the triage process, an analyst marks whether it is a false positive, true positive but benign, raised to the level of a security event, or raised to the level of a security incident. Then, you can use Jira to create filters on those level tags, and we're able to create metrics based on the alert type and the level and track which alerts are our top performers and which ones essentially create noise. We can also map those alerts down to security gaps and areas of coverage to ensure we provide a version of in-depth security monitoring. By having the case management aspect and using Jira filters and reports, we were able to automate one way of measuring success and metrics.

Use cases as coverage

Another way to measure the success of detections is to show the different use cases that are covered by the detections and map that to a risk registry and a threat model list. That way, you can show that you have some percentage of coverage for your environment and make more detections based on what is missing or a prioritization value. The problem is this has the possibility of encouraging a larger number of detections to be created over quality because, in essence, you can have a larger percentage of coverage with detections that create 90% or greater in false positives over a smaller percentage of network coverage with detections that have a 70% efficacy rate. Therefore, I tend to encourage using the first method of determining success for metrics so that you focus more on quality than on quantity. But this is a good way to implement the MITRE framework in your measurements because you could use different spreadsheets, charts, and so on, to show coverage. This could be presented similarly to the following screenshot:

Company Network/Security Control	Controls In Place	Applicable MITRE Controls	Percent Mitigated	Pending Actions	Notes
Strong Authentication to OKTA	Minimum Password Length Two Factor Authentication Session Lockout	T1110, T1550, T1098, T1136, T1621	4000/5000 (80%) of accounts have 2FA applied	Continue applying 2FA	Implement Organizational Wide Password Manager

Figure 8.3 – Chart to show coverage mappings

This is a simple chart that shows the aspect of the organization that is being looked at, the security controls that you should have or want to put in place, the technique codes that map to MITRE, the percentage of mitigation steps taken with detail, the pending actions that need to be taken, and any additional notes. Ideally, you want to include as much detail as possible to give.

Other ways are to focus on trends of detections and show the number of alerts triggered for different types of alerts. While this gives you an idea of your noisy detections, it is easy to jumble this metric and encourage false positives, which would hurt your SOC in the long run.

What metrics should be used

The tried-and-true metrics that I recommend using as a baseline in every environment are to determine the time to detection, the time to respond, and the time to mitigate. After this gets established, it becomes a metric that easily tells a story and is a way to quickly ensure that you comply with any **service-level agreements (SLAs)** you have established. It also gives you a potential goal in the future, which will allow you to drive down and improve those metrics to make your SOC more efficient. This effort can be easily presented regularly, and there are automated methods to gather those metrics. For presenting it, when we initially took the metric, we would use a red-yellow-green scale with the times. So, if our time to detect was, say, more than 24 hours, it might be at yellow or red, and green would be any time that meets or improves upon our pre-determined SLA. For automation efforts, we started with gathering these metrics for vulnerability scans, we initially wrote a Python script that would take vulnerability fields for vulnerability first seen, and vulnerability last observed, and the vulnerability would no longer be on the latest scan if it was mitigated. The script would scrape that data from an auto-generated Excel sheet and complete basic arithmetic to show those metrics daily. Over time, we utilized built-in APIs to pull the data from the source directly and edit a single Excel sheet so you no longer had to delete the historical data.

I have historically seen these three metrics as the core for most teams and they can be used for SOC triage, **network operations center** (**NOC**) triage, and vulnerability management, among other teams' work. I've even seen it broken down into detection types to show that some detections take longer to triage based on the potential finding and performing your due diligence. This approach to metrics also encourages cross-team collaboration efforts to work with the respective IT and engineering teams to work toward meeting those SLAs together regarding updating and patching systems. This metric can also be used to help justify additional resources. For example, if your average time to triage is 20 minutes per alert, and on average, your environment gets 200 alerts a day, that equates to 400 minutes or 66.67 hours or a full 8-hour day for just over 8 employees, not accounting for meetings or **paid time off** (**PTO**). If you only have, say, six employees, you now have quantitative metrics to help justify purchasing a **security orchestration, automation, and response** (**SOAR**) tool to help automate actions or hiring additional people, and if not, then you understand the risk that you are accepting with a potentially malicious action being conducted and alerted, and not being responded too.

Other types of metrics that can add contextual information but aren't the core ones would be to establish trends based on actions of sections of your network. For example, if you perform penetration tests, you can map out the tactics that were the most effective or network segments that resulted in the most findings. That way, you can track this over time to determine whether any mitigation strategies are effective, which would help prioritize efforts.

Even the lack of a metric can help tell a story. For example, if you are missing detections in an area, it's important to convey why. Is it because that environment is locked down and secure, or because you aren't capturing the right types of data flows to make detections? Both answers result in zero detections, but they tell drastically different stories. Therefore, even when you might not be able to think of a usable metric, there is still an option to use this to help establish the story around your detections.

Establishing usable metrics is key to telling your detect-and-respond story, no matter what it is. As seen, you can start with a core set of metrics such as *time to detect*, *time to triage*, and *time to mitigation*, and then after that is established, track more trends and status-update metrics to add to them. These metrics can be used as a way to justify more resources, as a way to highlight what a team does, and can be used for a quantitative approach to employee reviews to ensure that everyone is meeting the standard.

Summary

Detections and alerting are the bread and butter of any SOC environment, and it's important that you can determine which ones are successful and which ones need some help. You should look to set up a way to track the efficacy of alerts and audit the detection rules on a rotating basis to ensure they stay up-to-date with your potentially changing environment. After you've determined what does and doesn't work, you need to find a way to tell your story in a quantitative way that will help bring visibility to the risks, successes, SOC environment, need for resources, and so on. The skills gained from this chapter are primarily around key metrics that can be immediately captured within your environment and identifying good and bad detections. In the next chapter, we'll talk through runbooks and about what to do after an alert is triggered, and discuss the triage process.

Part 3 –
Continuous Improvement and
Innovation

The third and final part of this book is about triaging. You are provided with example triage scenarios, flowcharts, and playbooks. The intent is to give you practical knowledge on how to triage detections and how that can still be mapped to the ATT&CK framework. There is even coverage for how the ATT&CK framework can be applied to other teams, showing how universal it can be. It also covers ways to make triaging more efficient through the use of metrics, labels, and automation. The final chapter is where you will hear directly from industry professionals on where they believe the future of cybersecurity and SOC environments is headed.

This part has the following chapters:

- *Chapter 9, What Happens After an Alert is Triggered?*
- *Chapter 10, Validating Any Mappings and Detections*
- *Chapter 11, Implementing ATT&CK in All Parts of Your SOC*
- *Chapter 12, What's Next? Areas for Innovation in Your SOC*

9

What Happens After an Alert is Triggered?

Once an alert is triggered, a set of actions begins in theory. This chapter will discuss the different sets of actions, how to create playbooks, and to ultimately triage alerts, and examples of poorly created detections and their consequences. These are practical examples that can immediately be applied to your environments if they aren't already. This chapter shows off a variety of strategies for actions that can be taken and for creating playbooks.

This chapter will look at the following topics:

- What's next? Example playbooks and how to create them
- Templates for playbooks and best practices

Technical requirements

For this specific chapter, there are no installations or specific technologies that are required.

What's next? Example playbooks and how to create them

As alerts come into the **security operations center** (**SOC**), you need to find a way to streamline triage and have it done in a repeatable format. By doing so, you'll be able to scale your team because any member can follow a pre-determined set of steps to triage. That set of steps is what is known as a **playbook**. There are many different formats for playbooks, such as flowcharts and bulleted/numbered lists, and we can use tools to create playbooks with a native language or Python. We'll look at a few different options in this section.

Before we can even create a playbook, we must ensure we have repeatable detection types. This might mean that you have to break down a detection to be more specific rather than general or need to establish at least a few steps of what could be normal. It helps to have a senior analyst work with a junior analyst to determine the triage steps. The senior analyst will have insights on the right steps to take, whereas the junior analyst will help to ensure that there is no assumed knowledge and that steps aren't assumed. Once a set of steps or options are established, you should open the process to allow other analysts to test it and provide feedback. Playbooks can be used for most, if not all, situations, at least for part of them, and are critical to building a scalable SOC environment. You can even map any of the playbooks directly to the MITRE framework to help take the guesswork out of it.

Flowcharts

The first example playbook that we'll look at is a basic flowchart playbook. While none of it is automated, it still creates a knowledge base of steps to be taken when triaging an alert or performing an action, which will help drive down your mean time to triage. This playbook is important to tune to your environment because phishing is a common threat vector, and automating portions of its response can significantly help with analyst time. Phishing can relate to the following MITRE techniques:

- **T1566: Phishing:**

  - Spearphishing Attachment

  - Spearphishing Link

  - Spearphishing via Service

- **T1598: Phishing for Information:**

  - Spearphishing Attachment

  - Spearphishing Link

  - Spearphishing Service

There are other techniques. The following diagram is an example of a flowchart for triaging a potential phishing email:

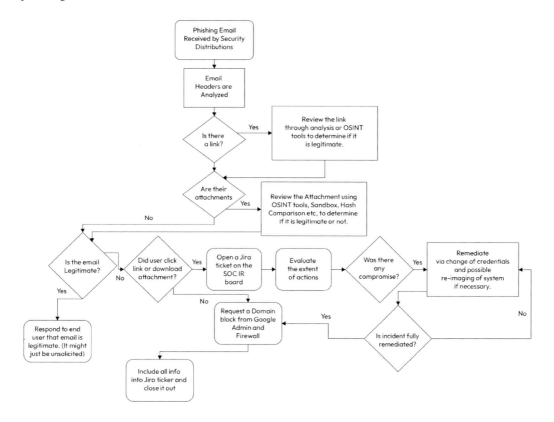

Figure 9.1 – Phishing playbook – flowchart style

If we start at the top, we can see that this playbook would begin when a potential phishing email is reported or discovered. The analyst would then take a look at the email headers, which can look like this:

Message ID	<63d6aaa091d8e_fd22abf7d086ce@8e4e3a8e-1-486f-9478-b9446769205a.mail>
Created at:	Sun, Jan 22, 2023 at 12:19 PM (Delivered after 2 seconds)
From:	Am@z0n < http://679699.com/>
To:	example@example.com
Subject:	Your Package for Delivery
SPF:	PASS with IP 167.81.24.133
DKIM:	'PASS' with domain zuppler.com

Figure 9.2 – Email headers

This is the top portion of an email header that you could use from your standard Gmail browser. Underneath this top-level information is the encoding for the email, which is where you can analyze additional links that are listed in the email. The analyst would review the domains and links in the email header and analyze them using an **Open Source Intelligence** (**OSINT**) tool such as *DomainTools*, *VirusTotal*, and so on. There are literally tons of OSINT tools and paid-for tools that have free versions (which is the case for both Virus Total and Domain Tools). When entering a link, you are presented with results that look like this:

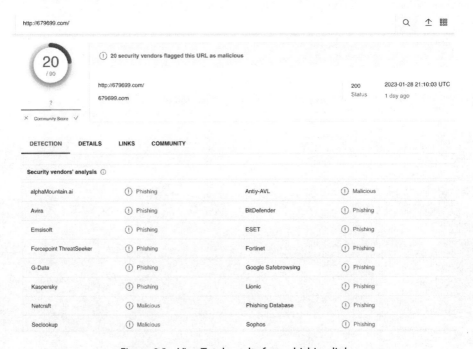

Figure 9.3 – VirusTotal results for a phishing link

As you can see from the screenshot, Virus Total found the domain from the headers to be malicious from 20 out of 90 sources. At first thought, you might think that that means 70 sources marked it as non-malicious, but it really shows that while some sources rated it as clean, some also listed it as unrated. It also shows that not all sources are the same, so typically, I'll take a look at what sources show as malicious, in this case, *Google SafeBrowsing*, *BitDefencer*, and *Sophos* are among them, and they are all legitimate, so I would mark this as malicious in our environment too. The next step, according to the playbook, would be to see whether there was an attachment; in this case, we'll assume there isn't one, and that takes us to the decision of whether the email is legitimate. We can safely say no since it is marked as malicious, and that brings us to whether any links were clicked. In this case, we'll assume not and can put in a domain block and send a notification to the end user, but if the link was clicked, you would open up a ticket in your case management system (*ServiceNow*, *Jira*, *Asana*, and so on) and track it as an incident to figure out the damage of clicking the link.

Runbooks via security orchestration, automation, and response (SOAR) tools

While this playbook lays out a set of common steps that can be followed for responding to phishing attacks, you should look to the tools that you have access to for security, as they might have outlines for playbooks as well. For example, here is an outline of a phishing test case for the tool *InsightConnect* from Rapid7:

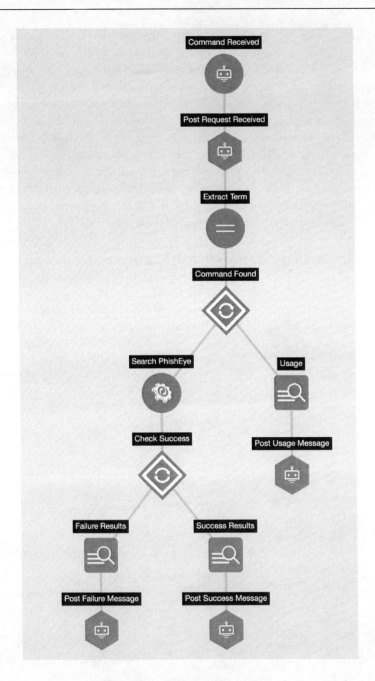

Figure 9.4 – Automated runbook

Another playbook that I've used in the past was based on a periodic beaconing alert. Periodic beaconing is typically indicative of a potentially infected system that is *phoning home*, sending packets to a **command and control** (**C2**) server to indicate that it is still active. Essentially, this alert was commonly triggering off instart, which is a service for Google Analytics, and you could figure it out from the URL starting with g001. In that case, we were looking to close the alerts quickly rather than have to go through multiple clicks. We also wanted newer analysts to learn what it was from the documentation so that they did not spend copious amounts of time triaging. So, we planned to ingest alerts into our **security information and event management** (**SIEM**), view the alert state (whether it was open, in progress, and so on), verify the signature of g001, and then close the alert with the comments that it was from Google Analytics and benign. We started by initially creating a confluence page in our knowledge base of the steps:

1. Find a periodic beaconing alert that is open and move it to the in progress stage.

2. Verify the URL for the beaconing alert.

3. If the URL starts with g001, close the alert with the comments that it is for Google Analytics.

This can be shown as a simple flowchart like this:

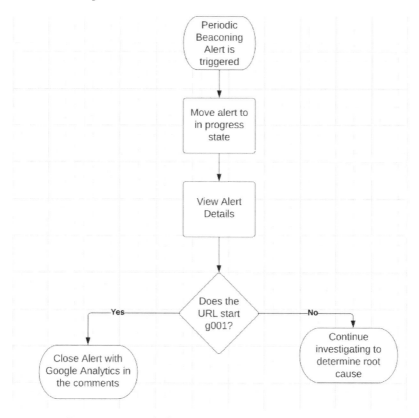

Figure 9.5 – Periodic beaconing Google Analytics playbook

For automation purposes, our intention was to utilize a two-way API integration between our SIEM tool and the product that found this alert. The rule would look for the same information as our flowchart shows, the g001, and send a response through that API connection to close the alert. Doing so would end up saving our analyst team an hour or two easily a week, which, while it doesn't seem like a lot initially, equates to 50–100 hours a year, and at a salary of $80,000 a year, saves between $1,900-3,850 a year on a low estimate. Small savings like that can then be used for other budgetary items such as buying training courses or team-building exercises.

Moving forward, some of the alerts and alert types that I would want to create runbooks or automation for are similar types of simple tasks. The reason is that a straightforward set of steps is easier to replicate in a SOAR type of tool. The first alert type would be actions for **domain typo squatting** alerts. Domain typo squatting is when a domain is registered where the domain is misspelled slightly so that it closely reflects a legitimate site, such as a site being registered as gooogle.com. Domain squatting can map to the following MITRE techniques:

- **T1583: Acquire Infrastructure:**

  - Domains

- **T1584: Compromise Infrastructure:**

  - Domains

This way, someone might accidentally add an additional *o* to Google and be directed to the fraudulent site. You can monitor for this by using tools or crawlers to search different domains and compare against a list of known domains; then, when there is one that is similar and not owned by your entity, you can be alerted. In the case of the alert, we'll typically grab whatever information we can on the domain, and if it is determined to be fraudulent, we'll send the information along to portals such as the *Norton Safe Web Portal*, and if the website is found to be safe or unknown and we have proof otherwise, we'll insert details for a dispute:

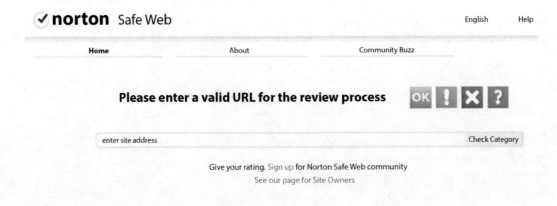

(a)

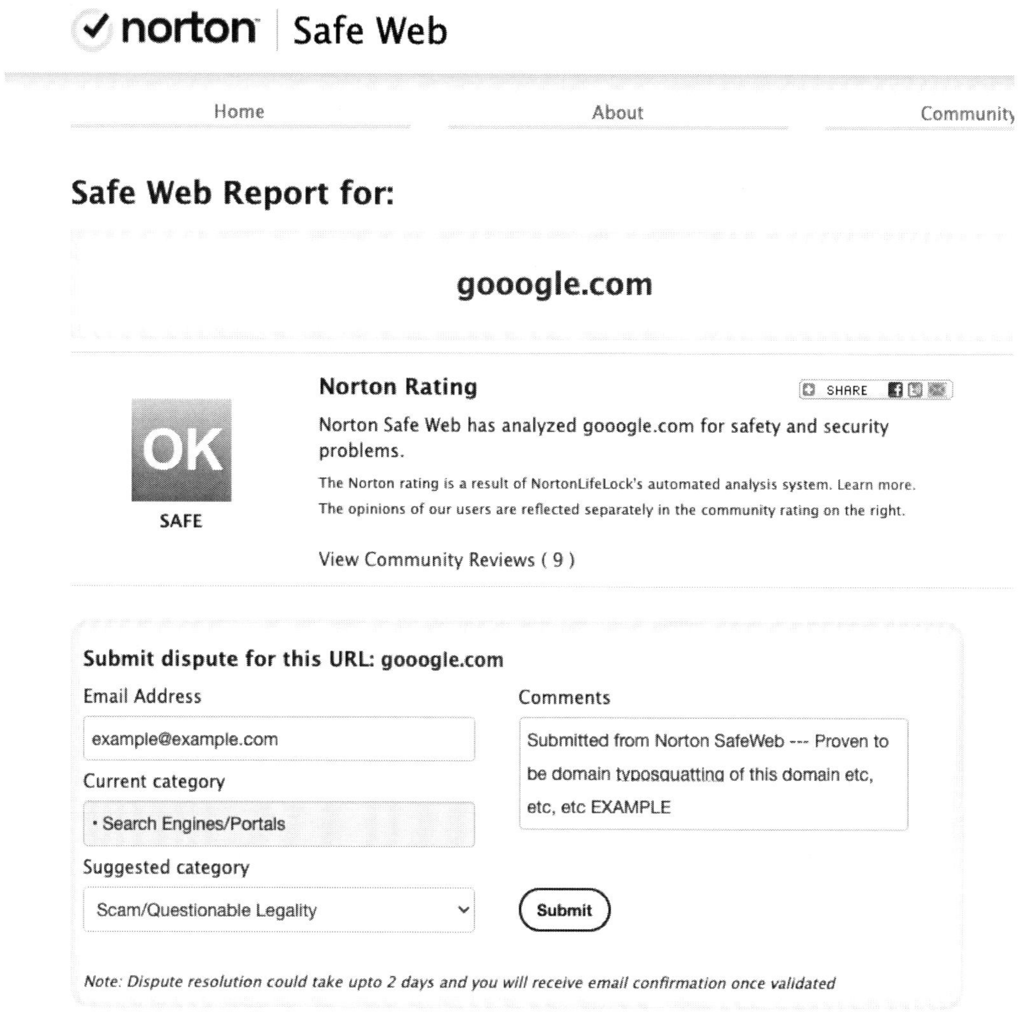

✔ norton | Safe Web

Home	About	Community

Safe Web Report for:

gooogle.com

Norton Rating

□ SHARE ■■■

Norton Safe Web has analyzed gooogle.com for safety and security problems.

The Norton rating is a result of NortonLifeLock's automated analysis system. Learn more.
The opinions of our users are reflected separately in the community rating on the right.

OK

SAFE

View Community Reviews (9)

Submit dispute for this URL: gooogle.com

Email Address

example@example.com

Current category

• Search Engines/Portals

Suggested category

Scam/Questionable Legality   ∨

Comments

Submitted from Norton SafeWeb --- Proven to be domain typosquatting of this domain etc, etc, etc EXAMPLE

(Submit)

Note: Dispute resolution could take upto 2 days and you will receive email confirmation once validated

(b)

Figure 9.6 – Norton Safe Web dispute example

If we were to write our triage steps in a traditional flowchart, it would look something like this:

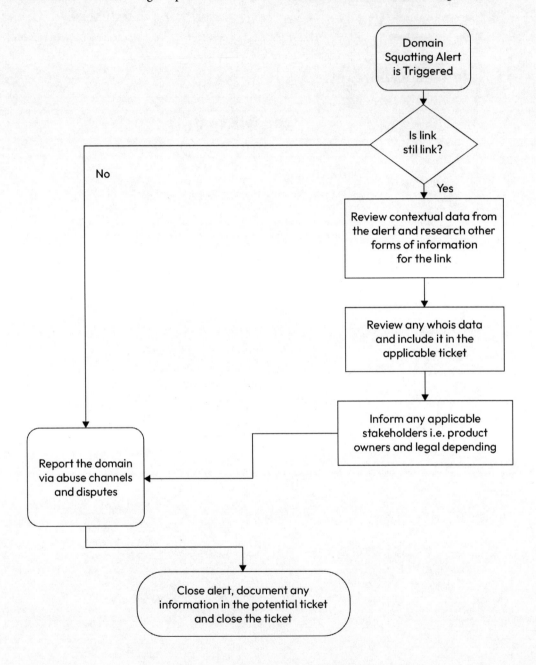

Figure 9.7 – Domain squatting playbook

In a perfect world, we'd start with this flowchart and, ideally, automate the analysis of the link, such as grabbing the WHOIS information. Then because all of our alerts trigger the creation of a Jira ticket, we would want any information to be automatically added to that ticket. Again, if possible, we'd come up with criteria for how to determine whether it is fraudulent, and if so, we would ideally send that information via API to abuse channels and implement domain blocks on our firewall if necessary. Even automating the information-gathering pieces could save a couple of hours a week depending on the number of alerts that have been generated.

The goal of creating any playbook is to start with a task that your team is already doing, then list out the common steps that are being taken. If nothing else, you should be able to make improvements based on the steps and create a repeatable manual process. The next step would be to create a flowchart based on the steps, which allows you to think through other triage options or rabbit holes. From there, you would want someone else to test the lists/flowchart to ensure that it makes sense. Finally, if you have the ability, you would want to automate as many of the processes as possible to make your team more efficient and allow them to work on other projects.

As you can see from this chapter, those are a few simple examples of the beginning stages of playbooks and runbooks, which would allow for repeatable, scalable triage of alerts that also coincide with alerts that have been matched with some possible MITRE techniques. In the next section, we'll continue to discuss playbook examples and best practices.

Templates for playbooks and best practices

As mentioned, there are a few different ways to create playbooks in a list, flowchart, and automated fashion. The first rough template I'll show is for ransomware. The first format is for ransomware that was found using an **endpoint detection and response (EDR)** tool in a list format:

1. An alert is triggered via an EDR tool (*Carbon Black*, *Crowdstrike*, *Sentinel One*, and so on).

2. Does the tool that triggered the alert have the ability to quarantine? If so, quarantine the system. If not, access a tool that does and quarantine the system. Coordinate with the IT team to possibly block the system via your **master data management (MDM)** tool, Jamf.

3. Open an incident response ticket with the preliminary information on the **incident response (IR)** board and establish a timeline.

4. Work with the IT team to determine whether any other Toast systems have been affected.

5. Set up a C2 comms channel in Slack or Teams, inviting your security team, IT team point of contact, legal point of contact, and other teams as applicable.

6. If the infection affects multiple systems, quarantine all infected, escalate the incident severity, and put out a **Public Service Announcement (PSA)** notice with as many details as necessary for how to avoid infection.

7. Review logs via the EDR tool to determine the file path of the infection, and review logs to determine how the infection occurred.

8. Save all logs that were used to determine the infection and save them in a restricted folder for evidentiary purposes.

9. Depending on the information that is compromised, recommend to the **chief information security officer (CISO)** that we employ a **digital forensics incident response (DFIR)** service.

10. Provide all logs as necessary.

11. Send out regular **situational reports (SITREPS)**.

12. Work with the chief legal officer to determine the legalities of ransomware and whether cyber insurance needs to be invoked.

13. Once approved, issue a new system and either issue a clean build or restore a backup. If restoring from backup, ensure that the vulnerability that allowed the infection is fixed.

14. Complete any remaining root cause analysis and close the incident response ticket.

15. Conduct the **after actions review/report (ARR)**.

Looking at this set of steps, a few areas can be improved for your environment. The first is that you would want to make it specific to your tools, roles, and so on. For example, if you already have a retainer with a DFIR provider, you will want to include the company and contact information. For roles, I prefer to keep roles rather than individual people to cover you in case someone switches roles or leaves the company. You should keep a directory of roles, people, and important contact information as part of your IR plan as an appendix so you know who to contact without having to search around. Make sure to review and update the contact list on a routine basis to ensure everything is up to date. Then, if you look at the steps, they are good at a high level, so they provide a solid template; however, you will want to make it as granular as possible or include other reporting options such as user reported, and so on. If you wanted to see this template in a flowchart format, it would look like this:

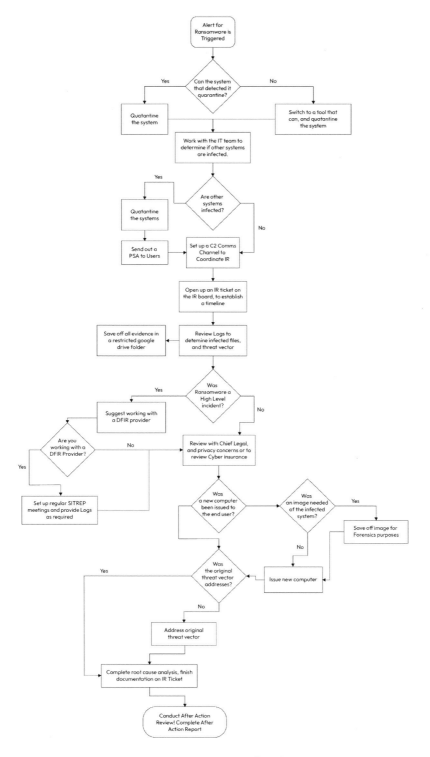

Figure 9.8 – Ransomware flowchart

As you can see from the chart, we start with the operation of an alert being triggered, and we follow the outline of the steps previously listed; however, the flowchart takes in the decisional options and flushes out the steps more. I prefer to include a flowchart with every runbook type so that I can run down the potential options and provide a hopefully straightforward path for an analyst to follow while triaging. Building out the flowchart also presents an opportunity for you to think through all the potential paths when triaging. Any time that you finish a flowchart, you should ask someone to triage using it, so they can provide helpful feedback about sections that might not be clear or that are left out. If you wanted to try to create a ransomware playbook in a SOAR tool, it might look something like this:

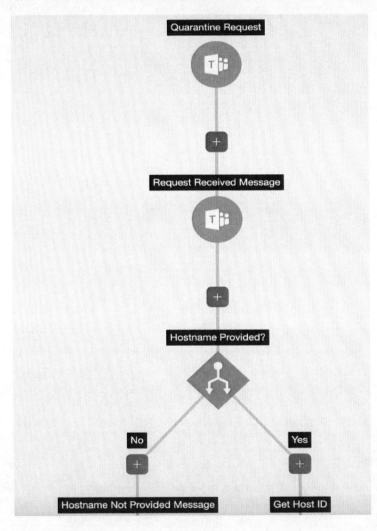

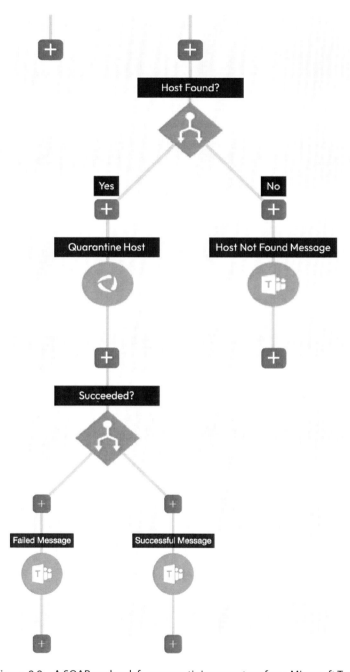

Figure 9.9 – A SOAR runbook for quarantining a system from Microsoft Teams

From the diagram, you can see a partial setup of a SOAR playbook. This automates part of the setup for the response effort. Specifically, this responds to quarantining a system that is identified. Due to the human factor, unless it's a cut-and-dry case, you'll almost always have to have some human interaction, but you should still strive to automate systems when possible. As you can see from this, the SOAR tool takes actions when a command is sent from Microsoft Teams; the system reviews the request to ensure it can gather a hostname, and if the hostname is valid, puts the host in a quarantine stage, and responds back to you on Teams to let you know the results. This action allows you to put the system in quarantine while you triage in a matter of seconds rather than having to log in to potentially multiple consoles and manually move the machine into a quarantine state, which could take a minute, if not more. That difference in time can be critical in an active incident; therefore, automation just makes sense.

Another potential runbook would be for threat hunting, more specifically around looking for specific software packages such as *Log4j*. Log4j is a Java-based logging utility that had a major vulnerability in 2021. The vulnerability allowed unauthorized actors to gain access through a remote code vulnerability and steal passwords, extract data, and install malware. Understandably, it's a vulnerability that you would want to patch immediately if found. Therefore, you could create an automated runbook that would notify you if a vulnerable version of Log4J was found on your network. It would look something like this runbook template:

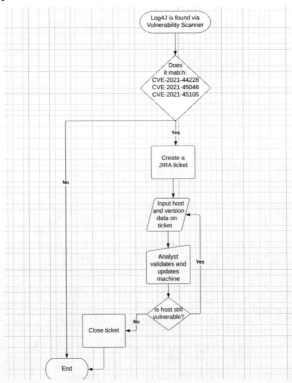

Figure 9.10 – Log4j runbook template

This template could be used as a SOAR runbook to automate quite a few actions. The first is, if you integrate your vulnerability scanner, such as *Nessus* or *InsightVM*, you can use the SOAR tool to review the results. You integrate a connection with your case management system, such as Jira, Asana, or ServiceNow, a ticket can be created, and the vulnerability information can be added to that newly created ticket. Then, you would have your analyst review the tickets and use your patch management system to update the impacted system. You can then use the vulnerability scanner to rescan the specific host and verify that it is no longer vulnerable, and use the SOAR tool to close the ticket. Therefore, at most, your analyst would have to validate the vulnerability and start the patching process; in an enterprise organization, you should be able to patch systems in an automated fashion. This would save your analyst the burden of logging into a vulnerability scanner tool and manually reviewing results when it even fits in their day. This could be the difference between patching before a vulnerability is exploited and having a crypto miner installed via that remote code execution vulnerability. It also allows your analysts to free up time, focus on critical vulnerabilities, and work on other high-priority projects.

An example of a runbook that could be used to help with a previously identified ineffective alert, in this case, take the instart one that refers to the periodic beaconing example; we can outline the steps for triage in a playbook format. Doing so will allow analysts to review and take action promptly, especially in cases where automation might not be possible, at least in the near time. A list of steps for triaging one of those alerts would look like this:

1.   A periodic beaconing alert is triggered.

2.   An analyst marks the alert as in progress and begins triaging.

3.   When reviewing the URL, it begins with `g001`:

    A.   The analyst performs OSINT research on the URL/IPs if needed.

4.   The analyst adds comments to the alert or ticket indicating that the traffic is associated with Google Analytics.

5.   The alert is closed.

There are a large number of templates in most tool's resource libraries that you can base your runbooks on. Using a template to start allows you to skip the first stage and just tailor it to your environment, which ultimately saves time. Looking through the resource library might also enlighten you to use cases that you can implement that you might not have thought of before. The templates will also help you triage faster in cases where you have to conduct any actions manually and can be applied to ineffective alerts to help drive down the amount of triage time spent on them. Some resource libraries even allow you to search for use cases that would find compliance frameworks findings, or findings that would match techniques and tactics of the MITRE ATT&CK framework.

Summary

Automating alert triage is a logical step in advancing your SOC environment and allows you to cover more alerts and actions. It will also lead to a faster time to detection, which will help you achieve better metrics and can make a major difference in identifying and responding to an incident. You can use the flowcharts, templates, and examples from this chapter and find others to quickly expand your SOC's capabilities and make it more scalable.

From this chapter, you should have picked up skills on creating and implementing playbooks and will be able to immediately implement these skills in your environment to help make it more efficient.

In the next chapter, we'll cover implementing different controls to cover for the MITRE ATT&CK framework in both your SOC environment as well as for functions of other teams, such as the **network operation center** (**NOC**), and mappings to compliance frameworks.

10

Validating Any Mappings and Detections

The most important step you can take to help yourself with creating mappings and good detections is by setting up a review process. This can be completed manually, or you can create an automated feedback loop to track the efficiency ratings of your mappings and make improvements when necessary. Whether this is necessary will be dependent on the fields that are captured when an alert is closed, such as **Value Added**, **Closed State**, and so on.

This chapter will cover the following topics:

- Discussing the importance of reviews
- Saving time and automating reviews with examples
- Turning alert triage feedback into something actionable

Technical requirements

For this specific chapter, no installations or specific technologies are required.

Discussing the importance of reviews

What is the purpose of implementing controls and detections without validating that they work in the first place and fill a need for your organization? In theory, you would only implement detections that fill needs such as mitigating risks from your risk registry and helping close visibility gaps, but sometimes it might just be about getting a quick win through tuning or trying to find the easiest detection to implement. Therefore, as mentioned in previous chapters, having a review system and feedback loop for systems is essential to ensure efficiency for both detections and your team as a whole.

To establish efficiency, you need to start with proper roles and responsibilities, which sounds simple but is a task that I still struggle with, due to ever-moving targets and tasks within the security field. You can start with a team charter, creating a vision for the team and a mission statement that helps identify the scope of the overall team. From there, you should create a **Responsible, Accountable, Consulted, and Informed** (**RACI**) document for your team and any teams that your team closely interacts with. Doing so will allow you to understand the roles and responsibilities of the team as a whole, which helps you identify specific roles and responsibilities of individual team members.

Part of establishing that will give you a general understanding of which types of tasks should be handed out to which members and allow you to predict how it will both positively and negatively impact your team. One responsibility that can be divvied out is that of reviews. This can be applied to reviewing tools for proper configuration, for alerts to see which ones are efficient, or identifying areas of your environment where there might be a visibility gap. That goes back to one of the key principles of security: *trust but verify*. In the case of the person, people, or team, trust that protections are put in place and detections have been completed but are verified through reviewing any ratings or closure statuses and providing a sanity check on the work completed. This also can be tied into the process of auditing.

If reviews are not completed, then there is a higher likelihood of improper detections staying active, potential detections being missed, and visibility gaps continuing. Therefore, next to actually triaging alerts, reviewing is critically important. The other aspect to keep in mind is that there are new security threats every day and the environments that we protect are constantly growing and changing, so yesterday's detections might not be effective anymore and you might have new security gaps. Therefore, as a team, you have to keep evolving, creating, and growing to keep up and get ahead if possible. The only way to do that is to regularly review your configurations, learn from them, and improve upon them.

Some of the review strategies that we put in place include the following:

- Using tools to automate aspects of the review and creating **subject-matter experts** (**SMEs**) through training for different areas of our network. For example, in an **Amazon Web Services** (**AWS**) environment, we might use alerts that feed off CloudTrail logs to alert on unsecured **Simple Storage Service** (**S3**) buckets or **Security Groups**, and as part of a validation and review process, we could implement Amazon Macie or **Security Hub** or use open source tools such as **Steampipe** or countless others to validate that the findings from alerts are legitimate and that no findings are being missed.

- Other options are to perform **purple team exercises**, whereby you can simulate attacks to test detections and responses as part of a normal validation process for detection and response. From there, you should continue to test your detection and response on a regular basis, focusing on high-risk areas of your network or new segments due to new **lines of business** (**LOBs**) or projects.

- Other than testing out detections and reviews, you can add fields to tickets to capture information that would be helpful when quickly reviewing. Some of the fields that we have added are around the purpose of the alert, which we titled **Closed State**, and around whether there was value added from the detection. In the next section, those two fields are explained in detail, among others. The idea is to gather as much information as possible to help with your review.

- Another option would be to conduct reviews based on an accreditation format or compliance standards such as the **Payment Card Industry Data Security Standard (PCI DSS)**, the **Health Insurance Portability and Accountability Act (HIPAA)**, or the **National Institute of Standards and Technology (NIST)** *800-53* standard, which gives you criteria to look for gaps, and you can align those with MITRE framework detections that are put in place, but basing checks on an accreditation standard might be limiting in some cases, as some standards are more rigid and might not accurately match your environment. You can also go down the list of MITRE tactics and review detections based on the framework, but a potential issue there is that not every tactic or technique will apply to your environment, and at times, new techniques and tactics might apply.

Whichever option you choose to conduct reviews, you'll want to find a balance between manual checks and automated checks as this will allow you to review a larger segment and be more efficient with what you review. Ultimately, it will help ensure that your environment is secure. In the next section, we'll review some options for automating portions of reviews and go further into how that can be used.

Saving time and automating reviews with examples

As mentioned, every security team should be looking to automate as much as possible to get more done efficiently and effectively, and reviews are no different. One way I recommend teams automate the review and feedback portion of alerts is by utilizing a two-way API with our case management tool, **Jira**. This starts with alerts that are triggered to automatically create tickets, which would look like this in Jira:

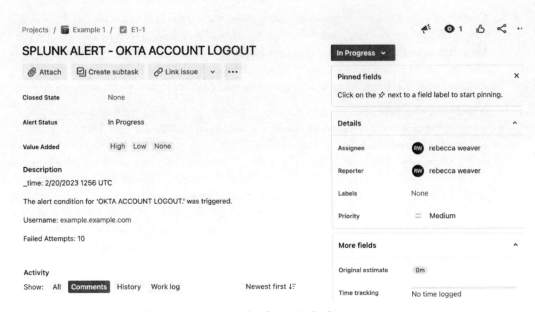

Figure 10.1 – A Jira ticket from a Splunk integration

On the preceding ticket, you can see the **Closed State** field—a ticket would be closed if it were **False Positive**, **Benign Unexpected**, **Benign Expected**, **Suspicious**, **Malicious**, or **Other**. Then, you see the **Alert Status** field, which can be either **Open**, **In Progress**, or **Closed**. The next field is **Value Added**, which would be a value inserted when the ticket is closed of either **No**, **High**, or **Low**, and we'll go into this in more detail in a moment. Then, there is the **Description** field, **Reporter**, **Assignee**, any additional labels (in this field, I typically add a specific detection name or tool name), and **Priority**. A ticket would be created automatically from an alert getting triggered—in this case, from Splunk. Then, this ticket would be in a queue for either an analyst or a **Security Orchestration, Automation, and Response** (**SOAR**) tool to begin triaging. Next, information would be added to the ticket, and after a determination on whether the alert is suspicious, malicious, or benign and action items were taken, the ticket would be closed with the **Alert Status** field changing to **Closed,** and the **Closed State** value and **Value Added** label being selected. For this specific type of ticket, as mentioned, we use **False Positive**, **Benign Unexpected**, **Benign Expected**, **Suspicious**, **Malicious**, or **Other** for the **Closed State** column. Here's a bit more detail on each option:

- **False Positive**: The alert triggered caused noise and the action was authorized and legitimate. This would result in no value added and potential tuning for the alert might be needed.

- **Benign Unexpected**: This could be due to a test or misconfiguration. It means that the traffic was not suspicious but was not *normal traffic* or expected, and could potentially be something such as a Google Analytics alert.

- **Benign Expected**: This is for traffic that could be normal and is part of a known feature, device, or software package. Depending on how often it triggers, you may want to consider adding whitelist options to cut down on noise.

- **Suspicious**: Traffic that might have caused a security event but not an incident that was a true positive, but limited action would be taken due to a lack of policy or other such reason.

- **Malicious**: Traffic that is a true positive that triggers an investigation and an incident response effort. These types of alerts provide a high level of value.

- **Other**: Any other edge use cases—something such as a misconfiguration or to align with any other criteria your organization might have.

The other area that has some ambiguity is the **Value Added** section. As a team, you would want to define this for your organization, but as a general rule of thumb, I mark no value for false positives, and depending on benign traffic, it might also be marked as **None**. Alerts that require an action or potentially fixing a misconfiguration could be low value (depending on the change), and suspicious and malicious traffic is typically high value. That, of course, still leaves a wide gap between each categorization, but that would be dependent on the details of the alert.

As mentioned, a ticket would be automatically created on the alert creation, and you can configure other tools such as Slack or Microsoft Teams to get notifications such as this:

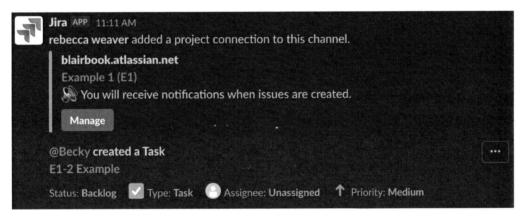

Figure 10.2 – Slack integration

This will notify your team's channel when a ticket is created so that an analyst doesn't have to stare at a Jira queue all day, waiting for tickets to be created. You can even send actions from Slack to the ticket itself, as seen here:

(a)

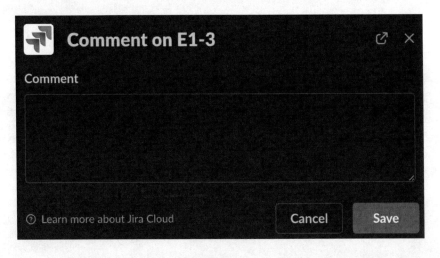

(b)

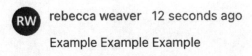

(c)

Figure 10.3 – Slack to Jira actions

As mentioned, you could also configure automated responses for triaging tickets through integration with your SOAR tool and Jira or directly through a tool that generates alerts. In theory, an alert would trigger, and then automated responses would be taken in accordance with your playbook configured to mirror your flowcharts, and the automated actions would either create or update a ticket and provide information in updates or in the **Details** section. In some cases, where the actions are clear-cut, you can even configure your SOAR tool to add the **Value Added** section or leave tickets in a final position for review for your team.

Through automation of actions, you're able to save precious time when triaging alerts. Automation also makes it easier for you to capture metrics that can be used to drive actions. In the next section, we'll cover which fields should be captured and what that data can be used for.

Turning alert triage feedback into something actionable

There is no point in collecting feedback unless you plan to drive action from it or are using it to gauge a response for a current action that has already been implemented. I recommend using **Value Added**, **Closed State**, and other fields such as **Labels** to both provide insight and try to drive/prioritize actions. One way to do that is to create dashboards within Jira, such as in the following example:

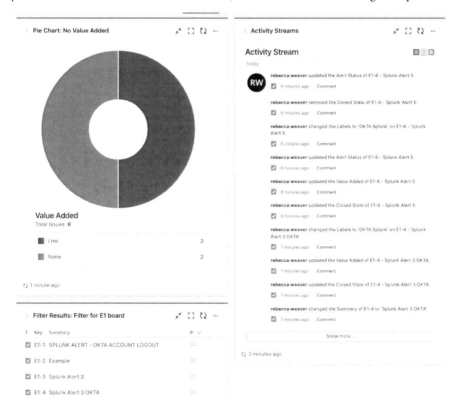

Figure 10.4 – Jira dashboard

As you can see from this screenshot, we have a very basic dashboard that has been created for a Jira project. This shows all activity on the board in the upper-right section, a pie chart based on **Value Added** for alerts in the upper-left section, and all current tickets in the bottom-left corner. To create a dashboard, you would start by creating a filter, like so:

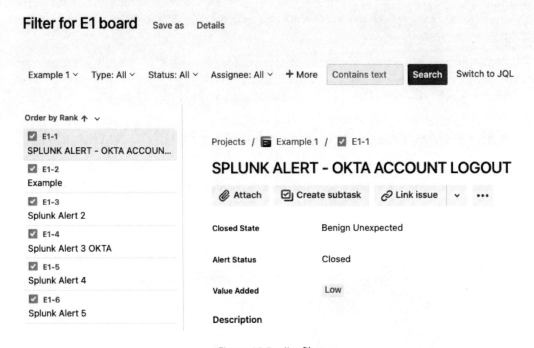

Figure 10.5 – Jira filter

You would first click the **Filter** tab up top and then you would be taken to a page like the one shown in the preceding screenshot, where all tickets are on the left and you can see various drop-down options to select and filter out tickets. After you have created your filters, you can create a chart by adding a **Gadget** filter on your dashboard, selecting the desired chart type, inputting the filter that you want to use, and selecting the statistic so that it would look like this:

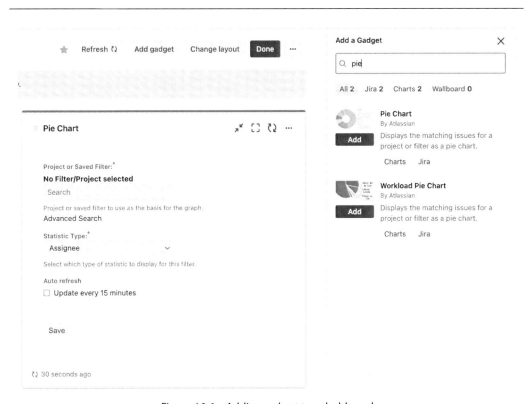

Figure 10.6 – Adding a chart to a dashboard

The point of a dashboard is to create a real-time way to view metrics such as who on your team assigned the most tickets, the average time to resolve a ticket, and the tool based on the label that is responsible for the most tickets. You can use this information for a multitude of purposes. For example, if you're looking at which team member has which tickets and notice that one team member has a significantly large number, you can then redistribute work, or the tickets they have might require less effort than other tickets. In the case where you are tracking ticket and detection type and **Value Added** fields and **Closed Status** fields, you might notice that a specific detection type has a high percentage of false-positive ratings and, therefore, has a large number of **None** values added. That should immediately trigger a review of the detection type to see whether it's possible to tune it to get a higher efficacy rating. Even in cases where, regardless of the **Value Added** and **Closed Status** fields, you can see which tools are being realistically used within your environment, that might trigger a review to ensure you are utilizing all the tools at your disposal to the best of their ability. It might also show areas where training for your analysts might be needed. There are literally countless types of metrics and narratives you can show from creating dashboards with filters when a feedback loop on alerts is created, all of which have the ability to drive actions for yourself, your team, and your organization.

With all of those actions identified, how do you prioritize? It depends. The following are examples of prioritizations:

- If there are actions that are tool-based around gaps or potential underutilization of tools, I have historically tried to list out the tools that are in the environment, gaps identified, the administrators for those tools, and the risks. Then, starting with the highest risks, I would recommend meeting with the administrator for the tools and conducting some research on your own or through company representatives to find out whether there are misconfigurations in the tool or potential features that might be included in your license but that you aren't taking full advantage of. I find that *underutilization of tools and features* is an extremely common issue, and most teams are quick to say that they need to buy the latest and greatest security tool; however, between open source tools and re-evaluating your tools, you can typically fill a gap or look for a replacement with confidence, all while being a good partner to your finance team. In fact, several years ago, I had the opportunity to travel and see hundreds of environments, and throughout that time, the underutilization of tools was found in no fewer than 90% of environments. Therefore, making the most of what you have will help free up funds for training, headcount, and tools that you might actually need.

- If the feedback from the dashboard metrics is showing *ineffective alerts*, I prioritize those actions based on the alerts that are the most ineffective and those that have the most potential. For example, I would prioritize an alert for account takeovers or an alert that might be for account lockouts because of the potential impact of the account takeover alert if it were a true positive, and because of other similarly related alerts that can act as mitigating controls. If needed to help determine the value, I tried to factor in a compromise that the alert in question might help detect, and whether it would be considered material or not. Material, in this case, would be if an incident reached a threshold where, if disclosed, it would have a negative impact on the organization. This could be a privacy threshold, as in the amount of data or accounts compromised, or a monetary threshold in the case of fraud or losses.

- If the prioritization is due to *workload*, I try to spread out the assignments based on the average number of tickets alerted in a 2-week period. In general, I recommend organizing teams in an *agile methodology*, where they work based on a 2-week period. You can try to plan for 60% project work and 40% operational work, with the plan to eventually even that out or switch it to 60% operations work and 40% project work. Then, start each 2-week sprint with a sprint planning meeting, typically a 2-hour session, to discuss as a team what you can commit to during that 2-week period, and apply points to how much effort each ticket will take. At this time, you can also assign alert types and triage responsibilities so that everyone can agree as a team that the workload is fairly split between everyone and that everyone will have clear expectations of which work will get done in that period. I also recommend holding a daily scrum meeting, only 15 minutes, to check in with everyone so that anyone can raise a red flag about a roadblock on a project, a quick update on an incident, or if there is an alert type or another type of assignment that is harder than expected, and adjustments can be made mid-sprint to help equal out the work. Of course, that all goes out of the window if there is a large-scale incident or another major event. In those cases, you have to push whichever projects need to be prioritized to assist as a team effort, and then pick up any work that fell off in the following sprint.

These are just a few examples of how you can use feedback that is captured on alerts and tickets to drive actions for your team, whether that be in the organization, creating new detections, or tuning a current detection that needs help. The point is that your team should always be striving to advance in their capability and maturity, and this is a way to help prioritize efforts based on quantifiable data that has been captured by your team and within your environment.

Summary

Feedback on all aspects of projects is important, and feedback on the value and ratings of alerts is no different. If we aren't capturing that information, then we'll never be able to properly understand our risks when it comes to detection, and could have a false sense of security. Just as with responses, we want to continue down the path of automating as much as possible in an effort to get a core understanding of our successful detections and of ones that might need a little bit of help. Understanding that will allow us to have a more operational team and help assist you in becoming more scalable. From this chapter, you should be able to critically look at your triage process and identify additional actions, such as steps that can be automated to assist with your triage process, and you should be able to add other fields to capture data during triage that can be used to drive actions.

In the next chapter, we'll discuss how to narrow down which alerts to implement and how you can implement security controls to cover aspects of MITRE for more than just a traditional **security operations center** (**SOC**) team and impact teams such as the **network operations center** (**NOC**). We'll also cover how to use those actions to create a policy and show more mappings between MITRE techniques and tactics with other compliance frameworks such as PCI DSS and HIPAA.

11

Implementing ATT&CK in All Parts of Your SOC

This chapter will outline how to narrow down your environment and prioritize where you need to fix a coverage area. The chapter will then list how you can implement detections and the ATT&CK framework as part of your overall security posture, and how it can be applicable to teams outside of the SOC as well. This chapter will cover the following:

- Examining a risk register at the corporate level

- Applying ATT&CK to NOC environments

- Mapping ATT&CK to compliance frameworks

- Using ATT&CK to create organizational policies and standards

Technical requirements

For this chapter, there are no installations or specific technologies that are required.

Examining a risk register at the corporate level

As discussed in *Chapter 2*, one way to characterize and prioritize risks is in a risk registry. The issue is that not all risk registries are created the same. That means that some are at a high level, some can be too granular, and some have too many fields, which can be confusing when calculating risk. In my experience, the best corporate risk registers have to find the balance between being technical and accessible to all stakeholders. We typically use the following for the columns in the risk register:

- The business organization or applicable line of business

- A description of the risk

- The score for the impact if exploited

- The score for the likelihood of the risk being implemented
- The risk score (impact x likelihood)
- The identified risk owner (can be a team or a person)
- Current compensating controls
- The date that the risk was first added

This allows you to gather all applicable information for a risk so that you can make informed decisions about which risks you are going to accept and which ones you want to target for mitigations. We can also tie those mitigations to techniques and detections, or technical implementations to the MITRE framework. We can start by looking at this example risk register:

Line of Business	Description	Impact	Likelihood	Risk Score (Likelihood x Impact)	Risk Owner	Compensating Controls	Date the Risk was Added
Hardware	End of life devices exist in our internal and customer networks. The following devices are non compliant: Windows XP, Windows Server 2008 R2	4 - High	5	20	Allen Ramsay	Monitoring is in place for devices. While we make a plan of action to transition away from EOL devices.	10/1/2022
Hardware	Hardware and System Patching does not meet our internal SLA's due to the End of Life software identified.	3 - Medium	4	12	Allen Ramsay		9/2/2021
Development Environment	Development Environment is not being scanned for vulnerabilities in our coding libraries.	4 - High	4	16	Emily Blair		2/3/2023
Internal Operations	The S3 buckets containing employee data are not encrypted and that could leave potential PII data at risk.	4 - High	5	20	Rebecca Blair	Reviewing the process to encrypt buckets.	2/23/2023

Figure 11.1 – Risk register example

This example outlines all of the columns that were mentioned and gives you a high-level understanding of the currently tracked risks, whether there are any controls, risks, and so on. We can see that the four example risks are **end-of-life** (**EOL**) devices; not meeting a company-directed service-level agreement (SLA) for patching; lack of vulnerability scanning in a development environment; and unencrypted **Personally Identifiable Information** (**PII**) data. From the risk scores, you can identify those with the highest level of risk to your organization, and in the case of a tie, you might have priority over a specific line of business. Overall, you can use this data to link to specific MITRE controls to implement detections and strategies, which, once implemented, could lower the risk score, and the applicable information would be added to the compensating controls.

For the first risk example, we can see that there are EOL devices in the corporate and customer environments – Windows Server 2008 R2 and Windows XP, to be specific. That lets us know that the *enterprise* is a Windows environment and that we need to use the applicable matrix. There is a multitude of different risks and techniques that could apply, which makes it complicated. For example, any techniques that can be mitigated by updating software might be applicable, due to the fact that EOL devices no longer receive updates. Some other MITRE techniques that might apply include the following:

- T1547: Boot or Logon AutoStart Execution: Kernel Modules and Extensions

- T1059: Command and Scripting Interpreter:

  - Powershell

  - Visual Basic

  - Python

- T1027: Obfuscated Files or Information:

  - Software Packing

  - Embedded Payloads

- T1566: Phishing:

  - Spearphishing Attachment

  - Spearphishing via Service

- T1221: Template Injection

- T1574: Hijack Execution: DLL Side Loading

- T1203: Exploitation for Client Execution

- T1190: Exploit Public-Facing Application

The selected techniques were ones that are susceptible to malware and buffer overflow attacks, which was a common criticism with Windows XP and Windows Server 2008. If we look at *T1190: Exploit Public-Facing Application* in detail, we can see that this technique is broad and it can apply to an adversary taking advantage of a bug or design vulnerability in an attempt to compromise a database, website, and so on. If we look at the procedural examples, we see the hacker group *BlackTech* listed. The group in question is believed to be a Chinese hacker organization, which was responsible for *CVE-2017-7269*. This exploit involved taking advantage of a buffer overflow vulnerability found in Microsoft IIS 6.0, a version that could have been used on Windows Server 2008. Depending on the content hosted on those servers, this exploit could be highly relevant. In the mitigation steps, we can see updating the software (which might not be possible), vulnerability scanning, and application isolation and sandboxing, among other suggestions. For detections, you would want to enable the monitoring of any application logs and network traffic.

The second risk on the registry is that hardware and software patching does not meet your organization's SLAs. This means that you are unable to update systems, which can leave known vulnerabilities exposed on systems. In this specific case, it's important to note that the issue is related to EOL systems. EOL systems no longer receive updates, which makes them particularly susceptible to this risk. However, it's worth mentioning that non-EOL devices could also be at risk, and this information should be included in the risk details. The following techniques from MITRE can map to system patching, and some of these might be applicable in this environment:

- T1548: Abuse Elevation Control Mechanism: Bypass User Account Control

- T1176: Browser Extensions

- T1110: Brute Force: Password Guessing

- T1555: Credentials from Password Stores: Password Managers

- T1602: Data from Configuration Repository:

    - **Simple Network Management Protocol (SNMP)**

    - **Management Information Base (MIB)** Dump

    - Network Device Configuration Dump

- T1189: Drive-by Compromise

- T1546: Event-Triggered Execution: Application Shimming

- T1190: Exploit Public-Facing Application

- T1212: Exploitation for Credential Access

- T1211: Exploitation for Defense Evasion

- T1068: Exploitation for Privilege Escalation

- T1210: Exploitation of Remote Services

- T1495: Firmware Corruption

- T1574: Hijack Execution Flow:

    - **Doubly Linked List (DLL)** Side-Loading

- T1137: Office Application Startup:

    - Outlook Forms

    - Outlook Home Page

    - Outlook Rules

- T1542: Pre-OS Boot:

    - System Firmware

    - Component Firmware

- T1072: Software Deployment Tools

- T1195: Supply Chain Compromise:

    - Compromise Software Dependencies and Development Tools

    - Compromise Software Supply Chain

- T1552: Unsecured Credentials:

    - Group Policy Preferences

- T15550: Use Alternative Authentication Material: Pass the Hash

If we can identify the systems that don't meet the SLAs, we can then narrow down the list of applicable MITRE techniques by focusing on those specific systems. If we investigate one that would more than likely be applicable due to the EOL devices, there is *T1546: Event-Triggered Execution: Application Shimming*. This is when an adversary abuses built-in system features such as a service that monitors for events – for example, logons or other user activities. The adversary might have the ability to gain access to a host system through repeatedly running malicious code and abusing those monitoring functions. One of the tricky parts is that since the adversary is abusing system features, it's hard to prevent with normal mitigation techniques. That is why it is recommended to upgrade to Windows 8 or higher. You can also attempt to detect it by creating detections to review file creation, modification, and metadata, as well as implement monitoring for process creations.

The third risk on our example chart is that there is no vulnerability scanning for the code libraries in the development environment. This means that vulnerabilities due to third-party dependencies could go undetected. Other areas for vulnerability scanning within a coding environment would be a **Dynamic Application Security Testing** (**DAST**) tool, which runs code and analyzes it for any potentially exploitable vulnerabilities. This type of risk can relate to the Enterprise set of matrices and can potentially apply to the following MITRE techniques:

- T1190: Exploit Public-Facing Applications

- T1210: Exploitation of Remote Services

- T1195: Supply Chain Compromise:

    - Compromise of Software Dependencies and Development Tools

    - Compromise Software Supply Chain

This means that if we look just at *T1195:001: Compromise of Software Dependencies and Development Tools*, we know there is a precedent set for adversaries to exploit third-party code dependencies and that there is a procedural example. In this instance, a backdoor exploit has been discovered, which adds malicious code to projects by manipulating files and folders listed in CocoaPods, an application-level dependency manager. As a result, the attacker can conduct ransomware-like levels of encryption on the host devices. Directly listed as a mitigating step is implementing vulnerability scanning. You can also implement monitoring by creating detections that review the file metadata for any files in your code base and verify that the hash for the files is legitimate.

The last example of a risk is related to Amazon S3 buckets that store employee records containing PII. These records are currently unencrypted, posing a security risk. Since S3 buckets are mentioned, we know that this is the cloud environment, we will look at the **Software-as-a-Service (SaaS)** matrix, and we know that PII is considered sensitive data. We can potentially map this risk to the following techniques:

- T1119: Automated Collection

- T1530: Data from Cloud Storage

- T1552: Unsecured Credentials:

  - Private Keys

- T1550: Use Alternative Authentication Material: Application Access Token

If we take a closer look at *T1530: Data from Cloud Storage*, we can see that this technique is when adversaries attempt to gain access to cloud storage, such as S3 buckets or Azure storage, to review the files and stored information in a possible attempt to leak credentials, potentially leak or sell PII data, or other nefarious activities. There are multiple procedural examples of an adversary group and the software it uses, which targets data from cloud storage. In this case, there are multiple mitigating steps that can be taken, such as the following:

- Audit the access to the S3 buckets

- Encrypt the S3 buckets

- Filter network traffic to the buckets

- Implement **Multi-Factor Authentication (MFA)** to gain access to the buckets

- Restrict File and Directory permissions

- Appropriate user account management

For detection, especially in this case, you would want to enable logging; since it's S3, you would enable **CloudTrail logs** and from there, potentially guard duty alerts for actions taken against the S3 buckets. Ideally, you would just review access controls for the buckets and enable encryption to be able to remove this risk from the risk registry.

That's how I would examine a corporate risk register and map the applicable techniques to the various risks. In the next section, we'll discuss some techniques that can be monitored by an NOC and what might be applicable.

Applying ATT&CK to NOC environments

When looking at the ATT&CK framework, you can see that there are **Enterprise**, **Mobile**, and **Industrial Control System frameworks** for different purposes. Under the Enterprise matrices is **Network matrix version 12**, with the following sub-techniques:

- **Initial Access**:

  - Exploit Public-Facing Application

  - Valid Accounts

- **Execution**:

  - Command and Scripting Interpreter:

    - Network Device CLI

- **Persistence**:

  - Modify Authentication Process:

    - Network Device Authentication

  - Pre-OS Boot:

    - ROMMONkit

    - TFTP Boot

  - Server Software Component:

    - Web Shell

  - Traffic Signaling:

    - Port Knocking

- **Privilege Escalation**:

  - Valid Accounts

- **Defense Evasion**:

  - Impair Defenses:

    - Impair Command History Logging

  - Indicator Removal on Host:

    - Clear Command History

    - Clear Network Connection History and Configurations

  - Modify Authentication Process:

    - Network Device Authentication

  - Modify System Image:

    - Patch System Image

    - Downgrade System Image

  - Network Boundary Bridging:

    - Network Address Translation Traversal

  - Pre-OS Boot:

    - ROMMONkit

    - TFTP Boot

  - Traffic Signaling:

    - Port Knocking

  - Valid Accounts

  - Weaken Encryption:

    - Reduce Key Space

    - Disable Crypto Hardware

- **Credential Access**:

  - Adversary-in-the-Middle

- Brute Force:

  - Password Guessing

  - Password Cracking

- Input Capture:

  - Keylogging

- Modify Authentication Process:

  - Network Device Authentication

- Network Sniffing

- **Discovery**:

  - File and Directory Discovery

  - Network Service Discovery

  - Network Sniffing

  - Password Policy Discovery

  - Remote System Discovery

  - System Information Discovery

  - System Network Configuration Discovery

  - System Network Connections Discovery

- **Collection**:

  - Adversary-in-the-Middle

  - Data from Configuration Repository:

    - SNMP (MIB Dump)

    - Network Device Configuration Dump

  - Data from Local System

  - Input Capture:

    - Keylogging

- **Command and Control**:

  - Non-Application Layer Protocol

  - Proxy:

    - Multi-Hop Proxy

  - Traffic Signaling:

    - Port Knocking

- **Exfiltration**:

  - Automated Exfiltration:

    - Traffic Duplication

- **Impact**:

  - Firmware Corruption

  - System Shutdown/Reboot

With a large number of potential techniques, you need to determine how to separate them for monitoring purposes. For instance, if you have an NOC team, it's essential to determine the scope of their monitoring responsibilities. Is it all internal networks or external networks? Additionally, what do the workflows look like in the case that something nefarious is found and it has to be escalated to a SOC or incident response team?

To start with, we can safely assume that **rogue devices** are a common headache for any NOC team, especially in a distributed environment. Rogue devices are any devices that are unmanaged and connected to your network. Due to the fact that they are unmanaged, they are typically considered malicious in nature, but the degree of severity would, of course, depend on what the device is and what its purpose for being on the network is. Some techniques that would apply to rogue devices are as follows:

- T1557 – Adversary in the Middle

- T1559 – Network Boundary Bridging:

  - Network Address Translation Traversal

- T1056: Input Capture:

  - Keylogging

- T1040 Network Sniffing

Although there may be other techniques that are applicable, depending on the network, if we consider an adversary-in-the-middle attack, we know that a rogue device connected to a protected network can intercept network traffic and funnel communication to other devices, depending on the network policies in place. This could lead to unintentional information disclosure, leakage of private information, remotely connecting to other systems and making configuration changes, and the list goes on. Therefore, this is definitely a control that an NOC environment would monitor. In terms of actions, depending on the network setup, an NOC would conduct the initial investigation and, if known, reach out to the owner for removal. If additional help is needed or there is suspected nefarious use of the rogue device, the NOC would then escalate to a SOC or incident response team for further action.

Essentially, an NOC is an extension of a monitoring team such as a SOC, and those teams should work closely together, and comprehensive monitoring and case management should be set up for the NOC team. The reason is that, depending on the size of the network, the NOC team has the responsibility of monitoring all changes to verify their legitimacy, they have the responsibility of recommending network changes based on data that they observe, and depending on their service offerings, they might even assist with hands-on changes. Their purpose is crucial from a trust-but-verify standpoint, so much so that they also work closely with audit teams to ensure actions being conducted are as they should be and can relate to a large number of techniques where an audit is part of the mitigation steps.

When working with an NOC, you should test its capabilities and response as you would a SOC with network-based purple team exercises; that way, you can ensure it is monitoring for the proper techniques, has the correct mitigation steps and detections in place, and that it is able to respond. For example, they might have the correct detections in place, but if data is only loaded once a day, then their detections are always going to be behind, so it's important to test their capabilities and make sure that that team is set up for success. Some monitoring tools that can be used would be normal SIEM tools, which pull in the appropriate network data, or dashboards for specific networking tools such as a Meraki device dashboard.

At a high level, you would want to ensure that your NOC is set up to review all techniques that are applicable to the **Network** matrix and ensure that they are being tested for efficiency, as without doing so, there could be real ramifications to your organization. In the next section, we'll map some of the MITRE techniques to different compliance frameworks.

Mapping ATT&CK to compliance frameworks

As previously discussed, there are a large number of compliance frameworks, and it's growing every year. In my opinion, the most common frameworks are the **Payment Card Industry Data Security Standard (PCI-DSS)**, **Health Insurance Portability and Accountability Act (HIPPA)**, **Global Data Protection Regulation (GDPR)**, **National Institute of Standards and Technology (NIST)** – **NIST-181** and **NIST 800-53**, for example – **International Organization for Standardization (ISO) 2001**, and **Service Organization Control (SOC2)**. Of course, as mentioned, there are other types of compliance frameworks that might be more applicable to your environment. With a large number of compliance frameworks, it can be confusing to keep track, so finding common mappings helps simplify it. In this section, we are going to map out a few different techniques for different compliance standards.

The first technique that we'll create is a mapping to *T1556: Modify Authentication Process*. This technique has seven sub-techniques, which are as follows:

- Domain Controller Authentication

- Password Filter DLL

- Reversible Encryption

- Pluggable Authentication Modules

- Network Device Authentication

- Multi-Factor Authentication

- Hybrid Identity

If we take MFA for our mapping, we can find that this maps to control IA-2 of the NIST-800-53 framework, which is for identification and authentication for all organizational users. We can also map MFA to PCI requirement 8.2 of the PCI Security Standards Council. Then, HIPAA guidance 164.312 lists technical safeguards, which include using MFA. So now, here you have a control mapping between three different compliance frameworks, and while the work would be manual upfront, you can document the mappings across the various techniques and the applicable compliance frameworks.

Another example of the technique to control mapping is for the *T1562: Impair Defenses* technique, which has the following sub-techniques:

- Disable or Modify Tools

- Disable Windows Event Logging

- Impair Command History Logging

- Disable or Modify System Firewall

- Indicator Blocking

- Disable or Modify Cloud Firewall

- Safe Mode Boot
- Downgrade Attack

For this list of sub-techniques, we can map some of them to apply to CM-6, which is for change and configuration management in regards to modifying or disabling firewalls. There is also a mapping to IA-3 for device identification and authentication. In PCI, it could map to control 1.1.1, which is to "*establish a formal process to validate and test all network connections, changes to firewall and router configurations amongst others*" (PCI-DSS guide). In HIPAA, it could map to 164.312(b), which is that "*firewalls must be configured to properly log and track all data on your computer systems that interact with patient information, as well as other firewall requirements*" (HIPAA requirements).

There are some blogs that have gone through and found some of the mappings, to help you along in that process, but I have yet to find an all-inclusive list of control mappings, so while you might be able to find some versions that would be helpful, it will take some manual work to put together. In the next section, we'll discuss using policies and standards to help mitigate some potential risks.

Using ATT&CK to create organizational policies and standards

A large part of having a mature security program is the policies and procedures. Unfortunately, that is one of the areas that is typically the weakest. The reason is that when standing up a new security program, there are so many priorities that your team starts focusing on the technical implementations, and before they know it, everyone has a different process for triaging, adding detections, and making security engineering recommendations. Fortunately, when implementing the ATT&CK controls for your SOC and other environments, you naturally have to evaluate and tune settings, and that is a great time to create **policies** and **standards**. The difference between the two is that a policy is a set of general guidelines or proposed actions. Policies can be more general and are typically written for compliance regulations; they show the intent for a set of actions that a team or organization should follow. A standard is taking that intent one step further. Standards act as more definitive rules to be followed, rather than intent. One example of a policy would be a *password exemption policy*. That would be a document that outlines how an exemption would be approved – for example, does a ticket need to be filed, who has to approve the exception, and what is the review process like? Whereas a standard would outline the minimum requirements for a password that would be technically acceptable, such as the minimum number of characters, what special characters can be used, how long a password is good for, and so on. As you can see from the standard, it is more definitive and can have technical controls that enforce it, whereas, with the policy, it is up to the user seeking the exception to have the right justification and is ultimately up to the approving party to determine whether an exception is acceptable or not.

As listed with all of the techniques, there are typically mitigation steps and detection examples that are also listed. At times, you might not be able to implement some of the mitigation steps recommended, and in those cases (and in general), you can create policies and standards to help mitigate the risk through user actions. For example, you can create a policy around using approved browser extensions for technique T1176. Or you can create golden images and standards for how to configure systems with the proper level of encryptions and updates, which would apply to a larger number of techniques. You can search for user training in the **Mitigations** section on the MITRE website, and that's an easy first step where policies, standards, and training can help mitigate risk.

Ultimately, my recommendation is to create policies and standards whenever possible so that the expectations are set, and you can update the standards and policies at least at a yearly rate. You also need to make sure all stakeholders review the standards and policies and audit systems on a regular basis to ensure that the policies and standards are being followed.

Summary

Evaluating a risk register at a corporate level, applying MITRE to other teams, mapping controls, and creating policies and standards are ways to increase the security standpoint of your organization and make them more efficient. As mentioned in the sections, most of these actions will require more manual work upfront but will save time overall. From this chapter, you should now be able to critically look at some of the non-traditional security teams and apply control mapping and MITRE controls to them, to help drive actions.

In the next chapter, we'll cover areas for improving your SOC environment to help increase its capabilities and make it more scalable.

12

What's Next? Areas for Innovation in Your SOC

This chapter will outline key areas that can take a SOC from basic to mature, covering topics such as scalability and automation. In this chapter, I will share my ideas for innovating my SOC, as well as insights from interviews with other industry professionals about what they believe needs to be done to promote innovation. The chapter will cover the following:

- Automation is the way

- Scaling to the future

- Helping hands – thoughts from industry professionals

Technical requirements

For this specific chapter, there are no installations or specific technologies that are required.

Automation is the way

As mentioned in other chapters, every team should be looking to automate as much as possible. Doing so will allow your team to increase their coverage and the number of alerts that can be triaged. In some of the previous examples, we've discussed using a **Search Orchestration Automation and Response** (**SOAR**) tool, which automates triage and response actions. These are tools such as **Splunk Phantom** and **Insight Connect**. They allow you to customize actions such as gathering information, quarantining systems, or implementing blocks. One of the issues is that not all teams and organizations have the money to purchase SOAR tools, so they must look to other options for automation.

One option if you have a coding background is to create your own scripts to automate different features. One example is when an old team member created a Python script that took the nightly vulnerability data, created JIRA tickets for the new vulnerabilities, and captured *mean time to detect* and *mean time to mitigate* metrics for updates. That changed the timely manual process of creating individual tickets and calculating the metrics into a simple process that was done by the time we even entered the office.

An area that can also be automated would be *approvals with constraints*. I've worked in a large number of environments where there were tons of *access approvals*, *approvals for implementations*, and so on. However, we'd like to look at setting different constraints that can be searched, such as justification, organizational structure, and so on, to automatically approve low-risk privileges without having to have a manual review process, which, depending on schedules, can sometimes take many days.

Another area that would be great for integration and automation is the *creation of new detections*. This is an area in which some artificial intelligence and machine learning tools are able to help. There are a number of current and emerging cybersecurity tools that are taking this into account, and there are even tools currently that have the ability to help write methodologies or rules – for example, **ChatGPT**. I asked ChatGPT to write a SIEM rule for cybersecurity detection and received this response:

> *"Here's an example of a SIEM rule for detecting a brute force attack on a web application:*
>
> *Rule Name: Brute Force Detection for Web Application*
>
> *Description: This rule detects brute force attacks on a web application by monitoring login attempts and blocking malicious IPs after a specified number of failed attempts.*
>
> *Conditions:*
>
> *Event type: Login Failure*
>
> *Event source: Web application logs*
>
> *Event severity: High*
>
> *Actions:*
>
> *Send email alert to the security team*
>
> *Block the source IP address after 5 consecutive failed login attempts within 1 minute"*
>
> *This rule will trigger an alert if there are five consecutive login failures from the same IP address within one minute. After triggering an alert, the rule will take action by blocking the malicious IP address to prevent further attacks. The security team will also be notified of the attack via email, allowing them to investigate and respond to the threat in a timely manner.*

Then, I asked ChatGPT to specifically write a *Splunk alert* to alert on *brute force attacks*, and received this response:

> *"Sure, here's an example of a Splunk alert that will trigger when a brute force attack is detected:*
>
> *In Splunk, create a new alert by clicking on "Alerts" in the left sidebar, then clicking "Create Alert."*
>
> *Under the "Search" tab, enter the following search query:*
>
> *index=<web_app_logs> | stats count by source_ip | where count > 5*
>
> *Replace <web_app_logs> with the name of the index that contains your web application logs. This search query will count the number of login attempts from each source IP address, and trigger an alert if any IP address has more than 5 attempts.*
>
> *Under the "Alert" tab, configure the following settings:*
>
> *Alert Type: Real-time*
>
> *Alert Condition: Greater Than*
>
> *Alert Threshold: 0*
>
> *Trigger Action: Send Email*
>
> *Configure the email settings by clicking "Add to Triggered Actions," then selecting "Send Email." Enter the email addresses of the recipients and customize the email message as needed.*
>
> *Save the alert by giving it a name, selecting the appropriate "Severity" level, and clicking "Save."*
>
> *Now, whenever a brute force attack is detected, Splunk will trigger an alert and send an email notification to the specified recipients. You can customize this alert further by adding additional conditions or actions, depending on your specific needs."*

As you can see from the responses, it's incredible to see what tools such as ChatGPT can do, and how it can spit out formats for detection and real-time alerts in a matter of seconds. These tools, in my opinion, will revolutionize the way all teams operate, particularly in the SOC, as they enable the implementation of numerous detections in a short period of time. Although the manual process of identifying prompts is still required, these tools automate the detection process.

The final part that I would automate and currently want to automate is more *threat emulation*. There are currently tools out there that already do this to some level, and of course, you have phishing tests and so on, but ideally, I'd like a tool that can test different aspects of our network, can feed in the data from either mitigation controls or analysts' responses, provide updated feedback on the current weakest points, and continue to do this on a regular basis.

There are a lot of areas to automate in any environment, and that will become crucial to succeeding as a SOC team. In the next section, we'll cover steps for scaling your team and how to enable to it grow into the future.

Scaling to the future

Scaling as a team is a concept that has always been around, but has been the primary focus of only senior-level leaders. In my experience, I've seen a shift in the past few years, and more mid-level leaders and individual stakeholders have been involved in scaling and roadmap planning. I've also, fortunately, had the experience of building multiple teams from the ground up. When creating the team, we established team norms, a vision and mission, and a charter so we understood the role of the team. When it came time to scale after making the initial hires, I loosely followed these steps:

- Evaluated the capabilities of the team members
- Projected out hiring for expanded operations and coverage and created an operations model
- Ensured there was cross-team collaboration in place, including policies and procedures
- Started an employee development and learning plan
- Filled our cybersecurity tool gaps

For the first step, *Evaluated the capabilities of the team members*, since I already had a charter, mission, and vision established, I understood what the overall responsibilities of the team were. I think I needed to figure out the individual strengths of the team members and, that way, I could determine who would be project leads, and what areas we needed to fill through new hires or training.

The second step of *Hiring and creating an operations model* has always been more complicated. Hiring is partially determined by the financial resources that your team has, but I'm also a believer in having metrics justify the need to hire. First, I had to establish metrics such as what skill sets the team was missing, what coverage we were missing, and so on. If you're an alert-based team, you can determine the number of alerts an analyst can triage and use the number of alerts that are left untriaged as justification. I also had to take into account an operations model. For my teams, I've always worked on a team that had some form of international support, whether it was a customer site or employees. I also knew that I needed to find a way to have around-the-clock incident response efforts, and while an on-call roster will work for a while, it's easy to get fatigued if there are a higher number of pages. I have also worked the night shift before in a SOC, and while some might like it, it wasn't for me. Therefore, the approach that I took was planning out what is known as a *follow-the-sun approach*.

This means that you strategically hire analysts in different geo-locations who can work what would be their 9-5 type schedule, and it is offset enough to give you 24/7 coverage. In a lot of cases, this is also a cost-saving measure for companies within the United States. Your coverage plan and roadmap should be projected out for a minimum of 6 months to a year, longer if you can, to make sure you are focused on the correct initiatives that line up with the business and can plan appropriately.

The third step is to *ensure there are open lines of communication with stakeholders*, such as other teams that you might work closely with, as well as to ensure procedures and policies are put in place. A large portion of scaling up for your team in terms of both headcount and capabilities is reliant on the cross-team relationships that are established. Therefore, with teams that I work closely with, I try to set up a biweekly meeting to cover any projects or to just keep the other teams informed of any of our projects that might impact them. It usually pays dividends to have those open lines of communication and is something that, if nothing else, I would strongly recommend you do. Policies and procedures need to be established to hold standards and rules for what needs to be followed from a security standpoint. For example, without an incident response plan being followed, every person will follow their own process and there is a high likelihood of missing something. Therefore, policies and procedures can be a sign of maturity in a security program.

The fourth step is to *create employee development and learning paths*. As a team that is growing, you want to ensure that you are providing opportunities for your employees to build their skill sets and help with their job satisfaction. It also allows you to help develop your employees to bridge some of the skill gaps within your team. This provides opportunities for mentorship and leadership, which can have a positive outcome for those employees and their careers.

The final step is to *fill out the cybersecurity tool gap*. This can be a combination of purchasing new tools, but it should also include making sure current tools are utilized to the best of their ability. It's extremely common for organizations to underutilize tools and look for solutions, whereas if they took the time to tweak their current implementation, they could save money. You want to make sure that you have price protection on any new contracts to protect your organization. You also want to make sure that you have a formalized process for conducting a **Proof of Concept** (**PoC**) where you test multiple tools, score them following the same criteria, and then you will have a high level of confidence when moving forward with your purchase request that the tool works for your environment.

Of course, there are many more steps or different steps that organizations might take, but this is the general outline that I have followed multiple times in my career. If there are questions or thoughts, I highly recommend reaching out to the greater information security community, and I have no doubt that you'll receive helpful tips.

Helping hands – thoughts from industry professionals

The security industry is surprisingly small, or at least it feels that way sometimes. It can also be incredibly welcoming to those looking to learn and insightful about what they believe the future will look like. I asked multiple different industry professionals what they believed the future of SOC environments would be, and their thoughts varied.

Ryan Franklin, the security manager of threat-hunting for Amazon in 2023, believes the following:

> *"One of the biggest challenges security teams face today is simply the reactive nature of our business. Nearly every team focuses heavily on detection and analysis, but detection and analysis do nothing to actually stop an attack. In many cases, ransomware actors are able to compromise an entire domain in a matter of hours. That leaves a very small window for our SOCs and SIRTs to take action, and that's exacerbated by other factors, such as visibility, coverage, and even alert fatigue. When we look to the future, we need to accept that the way we've been doing things isn't working and, more importantly, is not going to work. If we were playing poker, I would say this is where we should be thinking about folding our hand. There's no bluffing in security. If we really want to get ahead, we need to be willing to push the envelope, take risks, and try new approaches. Even if those things seem taboo by current standards, anything that can give our teams an edge against attackers should absolutely be on the table."*

Allen Ramsay, a computer network defense analyst for a government contractor in 2023, believes the following:

> *"Analytics and detections are going to eventually be AI/ML-based and mapped to controls such as MITRE automatically. This will lead to fewer SOC analysts' roles, but more security engineering type roles, in an evolution of security."*

David Cho, a director of cyber educational content for N2K Networks in 2023, believes the following:

> *"With the influx of AI /MI, along with better automation techniques, I believe SOCs will trend toward two main areas. The first is implementing new strategies that emphasize the data and analytics from more **Key Performance Indicators (KPIs)** that reflect the positive integration of automation and techniques. These strategies could be related to the MITRE Framework or something similar. The sheer amount of data that gets captured and analyzed needs to be pared down efficiently for use. The second area of focus revolves around the decentralization of SOC units. Rather, I believe that SOC functions will be integrated into various security teams within an organization."*

Kinshuk Saxena, a senior SOC engineer at a Boston-based tech company in 2023, said the following:

> *"For the SOC to evolve, it'll have to be more aligned with business risk and compliance, rather than just threats. Of course, it will still handle emerging threats to its organizations. It will utilize AI/ML concepts to handle the zillions of logs that are ingested and the amount of traffic from IoT devices. SOCs will have to get ready to triage and detect threats in real time and simultaneous actions will be performed as part of the incident response efforts."*

Jacob Berry, field CISO at Clumio in 2023, said the following:

> *"Today, the SOC exists for two reasons – one: technology produces low-fidelity security data; two: we must set a reasonable risk threshold to permit people to operate the business day to day. If we prevented or avoided all risk, businesses would fail.*
>
> *We will always have conditions in which we permit risky activity; therefore, we will always have a detect-and-respond capability in our security life cycle. Many future-looking statements on SOCs speak about full autonomy where detection occurs, a response is triggered, and an environment self-heals. The reality is that we need to perform a human-based risk analysis even in that fully autonomous vision. We will need to answer what regulations and contracts require breach notification. What is our projected liability from an incident? What was the root cause? Can we change moving forward?*
>
> *Technical analysis will change but detection and response for the foreseeable future will require humans.*
>
> *Let's look at an ideal future state: any detection means an incident is occurring. False positives are zero. The manual time spent analyzing data is close to zero. The challenges in achieving this vision today are rooted in the infancy of security data analytics. We often have the technology to generate information if a breach occurs, but the volume of information prevents action, or the information is too generic, doesn't have context, and is tough to decide on.*
>
> *The good news is, at the time of writing (Q1 2023), some exciting technology is on the cusp of helping reach this vision.*
>
> **XDR – Extended Detection and Response**
>
> *Today: XDR is much better than the old way of looking at all data sources independently. Correlations reduce some SOC tasks. Ecosystems are emerging that create SOC efficiencies. Most detections are still atomic.*
>
> *Future: Correlation detections and attack flows will receive more research and definition and become the standard. Interoperability will increase.*

Zero Trust – *Better verification of authorization*

Today: We are rethinking how data is accessed. With the enforcement of hardware verifying OS applications and identity being required to access apps and data, we are getting closer to having definitive audit trails.

Future: Legacy hardware isn't zero-trust-capable. We will need to get rid of legacy systems. Passwords need to die to allow identity management to change, making it close to impossible to compromise identity. These changes will help us create clear audit trails that make it easier to identify breaches.

Data, Data, Data

Today: Security data is becoming less disparate and less atomic. Big data and learning from datasets is challenging. ML in security detection often just reinforces what atomic alerts are true positives and to raise those to analysts more often.

Future: We will learn how to create better data synergy with our technology partners. We will have better datasets to train AI/ML models on to be able to identify attack patterns and abnormal indicators. ML functionality for detection will have models that can look at large security data lakes with much higher success rates.

AI

Today: At the time of writing, AI that can look at data and provide meaningful output, mostly based on text or images, is just coming to market. The improvements in the last few years have been massive and we are seeing a shift with a large impact on business.

Future: We likely will have AI models that can perform security data analysis for us, compare logs, and identify abnormalities that are actually breaches and not just IT doing uncommon IT tasks. Timelines for attack events will be able to be generated quickly and accurately. This of course relies on us getting the data right to feed the models.

Here are some takeaways for the future of SOC roles:

For CISOs

Centralize your data.

Make security data architecture work for your business partners.

Invest in vendors whose datasets drive the outcomes mentioned.

For SOC Managers

Ideally, in the future, SOC managers are IR managers. If we get closer to zero false positives, this is a reality. Additionally, security data managers may be swapped in for SOC managers.

For Analysts

Entry-level jobs might shift to security ML trainers and data analysts. Learn these skills now."

I even asked ChatGPT what the future of SOCs will be and received this response (ChatGPT pulls from data up to 2021):

*"**Secure Operating Centers (SOCs)** are becoming increasingly important in the field of cybersecurity as organizations seek to improve their ability to detect, respond to, and recover from cyber threats. As such, the future of SOCs is expected to be bright, with continued growth and innovation in this area.*

*One trend that is likely to shape the future of SOCs is the increasing use of **artificial intelligence (AI)** and **machine learning (ML)** to automate threat detection and response processes. This will allow SOCs to quickly identify and respond to threats in real time, reducing the risk of data breaches and other security incidents.*

Another trend that is likely to emerge is the increasing use of cloud-based SOCs. As more organizations move their IT infrastructure to the cloud, they will need SOC solutions that are specifically designed for a cloud environment. Cloud-based SOCs will enable organizations to monitor and respond to threats in real time, regardless of where their data is located.

Finally, as the cybersecurity landscape continues to evolve, SOCs will need to adapt to new threats and attack vectors. This will require a continuous focus on training and development, as well as the ability to quickly adapt to changing threats.

Overall, the future of SOCs looks promising, with continued growth, innovation, and investment in this critical area of cybersecurity."

Summary

The SOC team and environment aren't going anywhere, but they might look different in the future. I believe alignment with frameworks such as MITRE will be key moving forward to provide standardization, which will help teams become scalable. Additionally, it was a key theme that AI/ML and automation will both be important in growing your environments. If nothing else, please take away that you should be looking for opportunities to grow and optimize your environment, and never be afraid to reach out to the greater information security community for help.

Index

Packtpub.com

Subscribe to our online digital library for full access to over 7,000 books and videos, as well as industry leading tools to help you plan your personal development and advance your career. For more information, please visit our website.

Why subscribe?

- Spend less time learning and more time coding with practical eBooks and Videos from over 4,000 industry professionals

- Improve your learning with Skill Plans built especially for you

- Get a free eBook or video every month

- Fully searchable for easy access to vital information

- Copy and paste, print, and bookmark content

Did you know that Packt offers eBook versions of every book published, with PDF and ePub files available? You can upgrade to the eBook version at packtpub.com and as a print book customer, you are entitled to a discount on the eBook copy. Get in touch with us at customercare@packtpub.com for more details.

At www.packtpub.com, you can also read a collection of free technical articles, sign up for a range of free newsletters, and receive exclusive discounts and offers on Packt books and eBooks.

Other Books You May Enjoy

If you enjoyed this book, you may be interested in these other books by Packt:

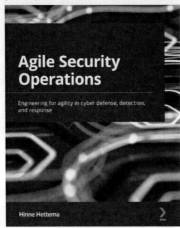

Agile Security Operations

Hinne Hettema

ISBN: 9781801815512

- Get acquainted with the changing landscape of security operations
- Understand how to sense an attacker's motives and capabilities
- Grasp key concepts of the kill chain, the ATT framework, and the Cynefin framework
- Get to grips with designing and developing a defensible security architecture
- Explore detection and response engineering
- Overcome challenges in measuring the security posture
- Derive and communicate business values through security operations
- Discover ways to implement security as part of development and business operations

Practical Threat Intelligence and Data-Driven Threat Hunting

Valentina Costa-Gazcón

ISBN: 9781838556372

- Understand what CTI is, its key concepts, and how it is useful for preventing threats and protecting your organization

- Explore the different stages of the TH process

- Model the data collected and understand how to document the findings

- Simulate threat actor activity in a lab environment

- Use the information collected to detect breaches and validate the results of your queries

- Use documentation and strategies to communicate processes to senior management and the wider business

Packt is searching for authors like you

If you're interested in becoming an author for Packt, please visit authors.packtpub.com and apply today. We have worked with thousands of developers and tech professionals, just like you, to help them share their insight with the global tech community. You can make a general application, apply for a specific hot topic that we are recruiting an author for, or submit your own idea.

Share Your Thoughts

Now you've finished *Aligning Security Operations with the MITRE ATT&CK Framework*, we'd love to hear your thoughts! Scan the QR code below to go straight to the Amazon review page for this book and share your feedback or leave a review on the site that you purchased it from.

https://packt.link/r/1804614262

Your review is important to us and the tech community and will help us make sure we're delivering excellent quality content.

Download a free PDF copy of this book

Thanks for purchasing this book!

Do you like to read on the go but are unable to carry your print books everywhere? Is your eBook purchase not compatible with the device of your choice?

Don't worry, now with every Packt book you get a DRM-free PDF version of that book at no cost.

Read anywhere, any place, on any device. Search, copy, and paste code from your favorite technical books directly into your application.

The perks don't stop there, you can get exclusive access to discounts, newsletters, and great free content in your inbox daily

Follow these simple steps to get the benefits:

1. Scan the QR code or visit the link below

https://packt.link/free-ebook/978-1-80461-426-6

2. Submit your proof of purchase
3. That's it! We'll send your free PDF and other benefits to your email directly

Manufactured by Amazon.ca
Acheson, AB

13967834R00107